Magic of Speech Evaluation

Gain World Class Public Speaking Experience by Evaluating Successful Speakers

Andrii Sedniev

Magic of Speech Evaluation

Gain World Class Public Speaking Experience by Evaluating Successful Speakers

Published by Andrii Sedniev

Copyright © 2019 by Andrii Sedniev

ISBN 978-1-07567-607-9

First printing, 2019

www.AndriiSedniev.com

PRINTED IN THE UNITED STATES OF AMERICA

Dedications

This book and my love are dedicated to Olena, my wife and partner, who makes every day in life worthwhile. Thank you for supporting me in every stage of development of *Magic of Speech Evaluation* system and giving encouragement when I needed it the most. Without you, this book might never have been finished.

I also want to dedicate this book to all past students of the *Magic of Speech Evaluation* system who, by their success, inspire me to become a better person every day.

Contents

What will you gain after reading this book?

What if you could get more public speaking experience after 10 hours of reading a book than the majority of speakers get after 10 months of speaking from stage?

After teaching hundreds of speakers worldwide, I discovered that you gain the most public speaking experience not from presenting to live audiences, but from developing the ability to analyze your own speeches and speeches of successful speakers.

In *Magic of Speech Evaluation* you will watch and evaluate short speeches of 15 successful speakers. You will also read an analysis of what made each speech effective and how it can be improved.

By the end of the book, you will have acquired the experience of applying the most effective public speaking techniques in various contexts. You will know how to improve each particular element of the speech to make it world-class from the first attempt.

In addition to gaining practical experience in *Magic of Speech Evaluation* you will learn public speaking techniques, used by 1000 of the best speakers in the world, that have the biggest impact on effectiveness of a speech.

Just knowing theory isn't enough to become a world-class speaker. You need the experience of applying public speaking techniques in different situations, and evaluating successful speakers is the fastest way to get this experience.

A month ago, my student Max said, "Andrii, from reading this book I gained more public speaking experience in 10 hours than from 10 months of speaking to live audiences."

Are you ready to begin a journey into a magic world of speech evaluation? Let's begin.

Why are TED speeches chosen for the book?

As you will notice, all speeches used in this book are from TED.com. You may reasonably ask, "Andrii, what is TED and why speeches from TED?"

TED is an organization that holds conferences around the world where speakers share their ideas from stage. On TED.com you can watch speeches of people who have invented a robot, crossed the South Pole, climbed Everest or architected the strangest building in the world. All speakers have a valuable message worth sharing with the world and often strong public speaking skills. There are several reasons why TED is a perfect source of speeches for evaluation purposes.

1) Speeches at TED.com are interesting to watch. Public speaking skills of speakers invited to TED.com range from above average to excellent.

2) It is possible not only to turn on subtitles for a speech at TED.com, but also to download the entire transcript. It may be valuable for content evaluation.

3) Speeches are not deleted from TED.com and the links to them are permanent. There is also an option to download each speech.

4) The way people speak in public today is different from how people spoke 50 or 100 years ago. Most speeches on TED.com were made within the last 7 years.

5) The length of most speeches on TED.com is between 5 and 15 minutes, which is perfect for evaluation purposes. The perfect amount of time to make one point in a speech is 10 minutes. No matter how long a speech is, it is a sequence of different messages. If you can effectively deliver one point, you will be able to create a world-class speech of any length. To evaluate how a speaker applies various public speaking techniques it is enough to watch how he or she delivers a single point.

These 5 reasons make TED.com an excellent source of speeches for evaluation. All speeches in this book were carefully selected and are excellent demonstrations of both common mistakes that speakers make and of effective applications of public speaking techniques.

3 foundations of public speaking

Many years ago I asked myself, "Why do speakers with almost no experience sometimes make much stronger speeches than some professional speakers?"

After many years of researching what makes speakers successful, I know the answer, "There are numerous public speaking techniques that can make your speech more effective, but not all of them have the same impact.

"Imagine that the speech is evaluated on a scale from 0 to 100. If you speak sincerely you earn 25 points, if you are energetic and passionate about your message you earn another 25 points, if you tell stories you get another 25 points, and if you do all the other public speaking techniques perfectly then you get the remaining 25 points.

"Because of their impact on a speech, speaking genuinely, speaking with energy, and telling stories are considered the 3 foundations of public speaking."

As you see, even if you mess up in all public speaking techniques, but tell stories and speak genuinely and passionately, your speech can still be very strong. But, if you mess up in 2 or 3 foundations of public speaking there is no way for your speech to be successful.

Sometimes beginner speakers give much more powerful speeches than professional speakers because they naturally use the 3 fundamental principles, and professional speakers use many other techniques, but forget about fundamentals. No matter what your age is, no matter how much experience you have, and no matter what your message is the 3 foundations of public speaking will make you successful on stage.

Tell stories

If you were a participant at the memory development training that I attended several years ago, you would hear a trainer saying, "Imagine that you need to remember a 10-digit phone number. If you try to memorize the digits by themselves, it may take you hours and eventually you will forget a phone number quickly because the digits are not associated with anything in your mind.

"However, if you associate digits with objects that are similar to them and then craft a story around these objects you will remember a phone number quickly and for a long time. And... the stranger the story, the more memorable it will be."

For example, your business partner says, "My phone number is 0-4-3-3-8-7-2-4-1-7." The story you create to remember this number may sound like this, "In the middle of a magic pond out of nowhere appeared a chair. A seagull that was flying around the pond landed on the chair. From another side of the pond came another seagull that also landed on the chair. The two seagulls really liked each other and decided to marry and live together happily for eternity. Luckily there appeared a swan on the pond who offered to be their priest. The swan took a clothes hanger out of his pocket and on the right side of it hanged a chair on which the seagulls were sitting and on the left a spear. Happy with his great work a swan came back home to his wife who is also a swan."

In this story 0 represents a pond, 4 is a chair, 3 is a seagull, 8 is an eternity and a marriage, 7 is a swan, 2 is a clothes hanger, and 1 is a spear.

During the training we learned how to remember foreign words, and sequences of numbers and facts, however all methods of memorization involved associating information with stories and visual anchors.

Guess what? In public speaking, the memory of the audience members works exactly the same. People don't remember what you say. They only remember what they see and feel while you say it. The only way to make your point remembered is to associate it with a story, a visual analogy, or an experience.

Because people remember information using images, the only way for you to tell a 10-minute speech is to tell a story and make a point. If you prepare a longer speech, then tell a story and make a point, tell another story and make a point, conduct an exercise and make a point, make a visual analogy and tell yet another point. If you don't use stories, audience members may enjoy your speech, but there is no chance they'll remember it. Tell stories and your speeches will make a lasting positive impact on the listeners.

Be genuine

Imagine that you sit in the audience and a presenter says, "I want you to be happy. When I see that my customers succeed it's the biggest joy in my life." In a few seconds your neighbor turns to you and whispers, "Is it just me or do you, also, feel that this guy is selfish and only cares about money and how much stuff he'll sell today? I don't trust this speaker and regret coming to this presentation."

Why is what the audience thinks completely opposite from what the speaker says? As a speaker you can control your words, gestures, and movements; however, you can't control nonverbal signals. Based on them the audience can see your true intention and if you are genuine or not.

When coming on stage a speaker always has a goal, for example, "My manager told me to make this presentation. I just need to fill 30 minutes and report back that the presentation was done," "I really want the audience to like me. I will try my best to appear likable," or "I just need to sell as many products by the end of the speech as possible. If I sell enough for $2000 I'll probably go on vacation next month."

Guess what? The audience members can read from nonverbal signals much more than you can imagine. Once they realize that you don't truly care about them, they will stop trusting you and the presentation will be over for them.

Once my student John asked, "Andrii, how can I appear sincere on stage?" I replied, "You see, John, you can't appear sincere on stage without really being sincere. Sincerity in our everyday life and on stage can't be faked. If you try to act out a better version of you – the audience members will notice it. If you don't truly believe in what you are talking about, the audience members will notice it. If you don't truly care about the audience members, they will notice it.

"The only way to make your audience trust you and accept your messages is to be genuinely interested in them and their success. There is a magic invocation that will ensure that you are sincere on stage, "People in the audience are the best people in my life. They are as important to me as my family or best friend. The only reason I speak is to give value, and change the lives of my audience members for the better. I will enjoy every second of being on stage and will make this presentation like it is my last one."

However to make this invocation work, you need to truly believe in it. When you prepare a speech believe in this invocation, while you practice a speech at home believe in this invocation, when you present to the audience believe in this invocation, and you will see how effective your speech can be.

If you genuinely care about the people who listen to your speech, they will genuinely care about you. Be genuine and very soon you will realize that speaking from stage can be one of the most pleasant experiences in the world.

Be energetic

When I studied at Michigan Ross School of Business in the MBA program, one day I was invited to participate in the event called "Startup Weekend." On Friday evening I arrived with several hundred aspiring entrepreneurs to one of the university buildings.

Within an hour everybody who had a business idea passionately pitched it to the entire audience within 60 seconds. Then by voting we selected the top 10 ideas and split into 10 teams. The goal of each team was to make as much progress as possible in developing a business based on their idea within Saturday and Sunday.

On Sunday afternoon the board consisting of representatives from venture capital funds, successful entrepreneurs, and university professors watched our prototypes, listened to final presentations, and awarded prizes to the winning teams.

What impressed me the most in this event was the energy in the room. I have never seen so many people passionate and enthusiastic about doing something new all in one place. And guess what? It was contagious.

When I left to go home after the final ceremony I thought, "Wow, I worked for 2 days on somebody else's idea for 15 hours a day, I wasn't paid for it, and somehow I feel happy, excited, and full of the belief that I can achieve anything I want in life. This passion, this energy, this enthusiasm in the audience is so contagious and I am grateful for it. Thank you, "Startup Weekend.""

I remember a particular day in my life when I totally fell in love with public speaking and also became a far better speaker almost instantly.

Many years ago I attended an acting training led by a famous stage director. One of the students in my group was 21-year-old Julie. One day the trainer said, "Now it's time to give a 3-minute speech that you have been working on during the weekend. Julie, you're first." When Julie went on stage she smiled and said, "The title of my speech is 'Fashion trends of spring.' This season, the polka-dot dress is popular. I like the bright colors…"

I thought, "It's amazing! Julie didn't implement anything that the stage director taught us. Her speech doesn't have any structure, she stumbles a lot, the topic is not interesting for me, but her speech is awesome! I could listen to it for hours!"

I asked myself, "What is special about her speech?" Then I realized, "Julie is highly energetic and passionate about what she is talking about and it's contagious."

When you are on stage, your energy is always contagious. If you are not excited about your speech, the audience will be bored and unexcited to hear you. However if you are energetic and passionate your audience will become excited and will think, "There should be something special about this topic, since the speaker is that excited. I will listen carefully to what he is about to say."

After my final speech at the acting training, a stage director said, "Andrii, your speech was impressive. You are a Julie, but in pants." I regard this as one of the best compliments I ever received and after this day make sure that in every speech I am energetic and passionate.

When I realized the power of being energetic on stage, it has dramatically improved the effectiveness of my speeches. When my students begin to take energy on stage seriously, they become much better speakers instantly. When you go on stage next time, make sure that you are truly excited about what you are talking about and I am confident that you will fall in love with public speaking and the audience will fall in love with you.

Every time you evaluate another speaker's speech ask yourself, "Does it include the 3 foundations of public speaking?" If yes, continue the evaluation to see how it can be improved even further. If not, make it the first recommendation to build the next speech around the 3 fundamental principles of public speaking. This advice will significantly improve the effectiveness of the speaker that you evaluate.

15 speeches for evaluation journey

How to watch and evaluate the speeches

How to watch videos

For gaining maximum value from the book, you need to be able to watch short videos of speeches.

At the link below you can get access to videos of all speeches from TED.com discussed in this book:
https://andriisedniev.com/magicofspeechevaluation/

If you are on the road, you can download speeches from TED.com in MP4 format to watch them later without internet access.

Don't forget that, in addition to video, you can see the transcript of each speech on TED.com if you want to analyze content in more detail.

How to evaluate the speeches

When I was 15 my family moved and during my last year before college I went to a high school which not only was closer to my house, but also significantly stronger in math.

I approached my new math teacher Alexander and said, "Alexander, I want to achieve the maximum I can in competitive math and I am willing to work as hard as possible this year. I know that you prepared several international level math Olympiad winners. Please suggest what I can work on at home in addition to regular classes."

He said, "You see, Andrii, to win a math Olympiad, relying only on agility of the brain isn't enough. You should also rely on your competitive math experience.

"I will give you books with collections of problems from past national and international math competitions. Think about each problem yourself for some time, and then read the solution in the back of the book. After a while you will notice patterns and memorize various approaches for tackling problems.

"Once you face a problem in a math competition you will have many different approaches in your arsenal to begin solving it and coupled with agility of the brain you will become a very strong contestant who can win."

The next day when I came home with about 10 books from Alexander, I took a stack of paper sheets from my bag and began thinking about the problems. Very soon I realized, "Oh, it takes me hours to work on just one problem. Each of these 10 books has at least 500 problems and it will take me an eternity to go over them at this pace. How can I become a far more competitive contestant in just a couple of months?"

In a few days I developed an approach that allowed me not only to gain competitive math experience quickly, but also to win numerous Olympiads throughout the year and be offered a place at one of the most prestigious universities in the country.

I tried to think about each problem for 2-3 minutes. If I had any ideas I thought longer, if I didn't I read the solution, and moved to another problem. With this method I could finish an entire book in one to three weeks.

What I noticed was that the approaches for solving difficult problems often repeated themselves and once I found the problem that required an approach that was similar to one of those I already knew, I solved it quickly.

During the math classes at school and during competitions, I was still working on problems completely on my own for hours, but the experience I was gaining at home raised my performance in competitive math significantly.

To gain as much public speaking experience as possible while reading this book I suggest you take the following approach:

Firstly, watch a video of the speech, think about it for 2-3 minutes and identify what was done effectively and what could be improved. Consider how what you learned from the previous evaluation may be applied to this speech.

Secondly, read the detailed analysis that follows a speech.

Finally, watch the video a second time and pay particular attention to the effective elements that were mentioned in the analysis as well as the elements that could be improved.

If you first think about the speech yourself, you will remember much better the insights learned from the analysis. After having analyzed several speeches you will notice that techniques that successful speakers use and sometimes forget to use repeat themselves.

By the end of reading *Magic of Speech Evaluation,* these techniques will become part of your personal arsenal. You will be able to clearly see what makes each speech effective and what can improve it even further. This ability will make you a more experienced speaker who can create a captivating speech from the first attempt.

Solely reading this book might not make you a world-class speaker instantly, however it will certainly get you several steps closer to this goal.

Speech 1: Richard Turere: My invention that made peace with lions

Access this and other videos used in this book here: https://andriisedniev.com/magicofspeechevaluation

The perfect story structure

A story is what activates the imagination of the audience members and makes the speech memorable. How you tell a story determines whether an audience will enjoy your speech and remember the message or not.

If you watch some of the greatest movies, theatrical plays, or speeches, you will notice that all of them are created based on a perfect story structure. The stories that use a perfect story structure keep the audience members engaged and excited and are remembered for years.

Your story will have the biggest impact if its structure is as close to the perfect story structure as possible. Richard's story is created completely in accordance with the perfect structure and is a very strong one. Let's see what the perfect story structure consists of.

Premise description

The perfect story begins with premise introduction. Here you can say where and when the action takes place, introduce main characters, and, if it is necessary, briefly describe their background. Premise introduction allows listeners to draw a scene in their imagination and then see a mental movie while you tell a story.

For example in Richard Turer's story, the action takes place in his village in Kenya National Nairobi Park. Richard introduces lions who kill zebras, himself, and warriors who kill lions and protect the livestock.

Conflict

Right after the premise description the conflict needs to be introduced to provoke curiosity of the listeners. Conflict creates questions in the minds of the audience members such as, "What will the character do next? How will this conflict be resolved?"

In Richard's speech conflict is introduced right after the premise and can be summarized in the following way, "Lions kill the livestock of the village dwellers and Moran warriors kill lions. On one hand people of Masai suffer because their livestock is killed, but on the other hand the Nairobi Park suffers because there are very few lions left."

Conflict makes audience members curious to hear a story and a resolution in the end. If your story has a conflict, the audience will be excited to learn what will happen next and their attention will be yours during the entire speech.

Conflict escalation

Once a conflict is introduced, escalate it, and increase tension in the story until it reaches the climax. For example, "Richard first tried to scare the lions using fire. It didn't work. Next he came up with an idea to scare the lions with a scarecrow, but it worked only for one day, and still didn't solve the problem of protecting the livestock."

If after announcing the conflict you give a resolution right away, the audience may not be yet interested to hear it.

However, if you let the audience suffer with the character and feel the frustration they will be eager to learn a resolution in the end and will remember the story for a long time.

Climax

A climax scene is the most exciting and critical part of the story because it shows how a conflict is finally resolved. Show the climax scene in detail so that audience members can clearly see it in their imagination.

For example, instead of just saying, "I figured out that lions are scared of the moving light, so I assembled the blinking torch and it solved the issue with lions in my village," Richard lets listeners clearly see the resolution of the conflict. You can see how exactly Richard learned electronics, how he assembled the blinking torches, and what the lions saw near the cowshed.

Conclusion

The goal of every story is to illustrate a point that a speaker associated it with. If in conclusion a point is tied to a story, it will be remembered for a long time and sometimes it will change the lives of the audience members for the better. In Richard's story the point was: "I used to hate lions, but after my invention we are able to co-exist with lions without conflict."

People always remember best what they hear last. The conclusion is perhaps the most important part of the speech because it gives value to the audience members and lets them remember a takeaway message.

Stories are easy to remember because they provoke the imagination of the audience. The perfect story structure proved to be the most effective structure not only in public speaking, but also in written stories, movies, and theatrical plays. Use all or most of the perfect story structure components and your story will become as powerful as possible.

Use of PowerPoint

The main purpose of slides is to make a speech more visual. The most effective way to construct a slide is to just use a single photo or a scheme on the entire slide. Pictures help audience members to draw a scene of the story in their imaginations.

As you saw, Richard used photos of his village, lions, warriors, and killed livestock, and they helped to make the story more visual, interesting, and memorable for the audience.

If you watch TED.com a lot, you may notice that most speakers just use a single photo or a picture per slide because it's effective.

When you create a slide, avoid text. Why? People can't simultaneously read and listen to a speaker. If you decide that text is necessary, don't use more than 8 words per slide in order to not compete with PowerPoint for attention.

Dialogue

Dialogue breathes life into a story because it allows the audience to see actions happen right in front of their eyes instead of hearing narration about events from the past.

Dialogue is one of the most powerful components of the story, because it makes the audience members engaged and excited to hear the speech and see the story development on stage.

Richard excellently puts the words of the characters in dialogue, "She asked me if I can put the lights for her, and I said, 'Yes.'" Even the short word "Yes" said in the form of dialogue makes a story livelier.

"The second day the lions would come back and say, 'This thing is not moving, it's always here.'" This phrase puts the words of the lions into dialogue. This phrase not only made the story livelier but also made the audience laugh. Animals and inanimate objects can also speak in dialogue, and when they do it's often funny.

If there is no dialogue your speech is just a news report but not a speech. However, if your speech includes only dialogue, it's not a speech either. It's a theatrical play. Your goal as a speaker is to find a proper balance between narration and dialogue. Since almost all speakers don't have enough dialogue in their speech, simply adding more dialogue usually helps to reach the perfect balance. How can the concentration of dialogue be increased in Richard's speech?

Firstly, instead of saying, "The first idea I got was to use fire because I thought lions were scared of fire," Richard can say, "An idea popped up in my head, 'Hey, I guess I heard somewhere that lions are scared of fire. I'll use fire to scare them.'"

Instead of "A second idea I got was to use a scarecrow. I was trying to trick the lions into thinking that I was standing near the cowshed," he can say, "Then I had a second idea,

'I'll trick the lions. I will use the scarecrow to make them think that I am standing near the cowshed.'"

Always tell your own thoughts and thoughts of other characters in the form of dialogue. When you allow the audience to hear what you are thinking, they will not just get more engaged into a story, but will also trust you more.

Secondly, we can turn a phrase, "She asked me if I can put the lights for her and I said, 'Yes'," into "She asked me, 'Richie, can you put the lights for me?' 'Yes.'" Putting the words of grandma in a form of dialogue makes this conversation livelier.

The second rule is that whenever characters talk in a story, put their lines in the form of dialogue. In an article you can write, "When I entered my manager's office he told me to close the door," but in a speech it should always be "When I entered my manager's office he said, 'Please close the door, Andrii.'"

Richard effectively used dialogue, however turning the thoughts and lines of the characters into a form of dialogue can make the speech even more captivating.

Don't interrupt the audience

Any activity from the audience such as applause or laughter can be considered as audience talking. Imagine that each time you try to tell something, you are interrupted by a friend. After a couple of interruptions you may not only have no desire to speak, but also no desire to listen to the friend.

The same happens with the audience members if you don't notice their applause or laughter and just continue talking.

After a while they will not only avoid reacting, but will also stop listening.

Richard started speaking only after the audience's applause stopped. Every time the audience laughed he made a pause and continued only after the laughter stopped. These pauses added a conversational feel to the speech and weight to Richard's words.

When the audience sees that you hear them, your speech becomes a conversation and you – nice company. There are many speakers who never interrupt people during one-on-one conversation, but do unintentionally interrupt their audiences and lose attention. Don't be one of them.

Contrast

Contrast is important for a speech to be effective because whenever an audience member notices any pattern in your delivery he or she becomes less attentive. People will be thinking about their issues at home, about the work they need to complete tomorrow, or just daydreaming. If you want full attention from the audience avoid creating patterns in speech delivery.

Change the pace of the speech, the volume of your voice, and use pauses. Make different gestures, movements, and vary your energy. Change everything you can, break all patterns, and the audience's attention will be yours during the entire speech.

In terms of contrast Richard does pause after important points and interchanges gestures with the resting position for his hands. Varying the pace of speaking and volume of voice can break additional patterns and help to hold the attention of the audience even better.

Gestures

When Richard finished each of the gestures his hands were hanging relaxed along the body. It's the only resting position that is natural during a conversation or a speech.

Sometimes speakers hold fingers crossed in front of them, just as soccer players do before the penalty kick. Sometimes speakers put the fingers of each palm together, so that they form a pyramid, and hold their hands at the stomach level. These and other versions are distracting for the audience and convey a message that a speaker doesn't feel confident.

Where are your hands when you are walking? Where are your hands when you speak during a one-on-one conversation? Correct. They are relaxed and hanging along the body.

When you finish a gesture, always return your hands to the natural resting position. Don't invent any new ones.

To improve:

Gestures in the speech about lions will become more effective if they are broader and more versatile. Broad gestures are more visual and convey a message that the speaker is genuine and confident. When gestures are varied and illustrate actions in a story, they make it much more visual. The main purpose of gestures, just like the purpose of the slides, props, and videos, is to make a speech more visual for the audience and hence more memorable.

Props (Lion lights)

The goal of the speaker is to make a speech as visual as possible on stage, so that it is remembered by the audience.

In his speech Richard turned off the light in the audience and showed the blinking lights that the lions saw near the cowshed. This allowed the audience not only to see the story visually, but also to feel themselves a part of it.

Be creative about how you can make the speech an exciting experience for the audience members, and chances are that they will remember it forever.

Be succinct

One of the reasons why TED.com was selected as a source of speeches for evaluation is that it provides a full transcript for each speech. If you listen carefully to Richard's speech or read the transcript you will notice that all sentences in it are important.

You can't throw away any sentence without detracting value from a story. This makes Richard's speech highly succinct, this allows the story to develop quickly and to cover a lot of information within just 7 minutes, while keeping the audience fully engaged.

Every sentence either adds to or detracts from the value of the speech and there is no middle point. Ask yourself, "Is this sentence critical for conveying my message? Does it make action in a story move forward?"

If a speech can exist without a particular sentence, this sentence makes a message less clear and a speech less valuable. If your speech doesn't lose any value after cutting out a particular sentence, remove it, and the value of the speech will increase. Always make sure that your speech is succinct and listeners will truly appreciate it.

Overall, Richard's speech is one of the best ones I have heard in the past year. Richard is just 13 years old, and English isn't his first language yet his speech is more powerful than most speeches I heard from professional speakers. The effectiveness of a speaker doesn't depend as much on the amount of hours spent on stage, as on how he or she uses the fundamental principles of public speaking.

Speech 2: Tyler DeWitt: Hey, science teachers – make it fun!

Access this and other videos used in this book here: https://andriisedniev.com/magicofspeechevaluation

Helen's story

One year ago my student Helen asked, "Andrii, I work at one of the major USA pharmaceutical producers and often make technical presentations for pharmacists. Is there a way I can craft my presentation using stories?"

"Absolutely, Helen. When you make a technical speech and want it to be understood and remembered, you need to connect what the audience members don't know with what they do know and can imagine.

"For example, 'If a bacterium is a plant, then DNA is a blueprint that tells its workers what to produce.'

"Imagine that a virus is a secret agent that penetrates the plant at night and rewrites the blueprint on the main computer. When workers come in the morning, they realize that now they need to produce viruses instead of new bacteria.

"People can't imagine DNA or a virus, however they can easily imagine a secret agent, a computer, or a plant. If you associate technical concepts with visual pictures and make a story around them, the audience will be excited to hear your speech and will remember your message for a long time.

"I will send you a link to the speech of Tyler Dewitt so that you can see how he describes scientific concepts using analogies and stories."

Two months later I received a call from Helen, "Andrii, Andrii, you won't believe it. After the presentation I made using analogies and stories, pharmacists not only remember almost everything I talked about but also say that it was perhaps the best presentation they have heard from any of the pharmaceutical producers. Now when our company invites pharmacy chains for the event they particularly ask me to be a presenter."

No matter how serious, technical, or important your presentation is the public speaking principles don't change. People only remember what they can see, touch, or smell in their imagination or real life.

Make a speech visual

One of the fundamental rules in public speaking is: always tie a point to a visual anchor. Audience members don't remember what you say. They only remember what they see and feel while you say it.

The speech "Hey, science teachers – make it fun!" is very easy to remember because Tyler used stories and analogies as anchors. For example Tyler told a story about what happened to him in a classroom as a teacher and a horror story about viruses.

"Virus DNA takes control of the cell and tells it to create more viruses. It's like going to a car factory and replacing the blueprints." This analogy helped to tie unknown information to the known one. Students might not be able to imagine what happens inside the cell, but they can easily imagine a car factory.

In his speech Tyler excellently used a story and analogy as visual anchors. In the next speech about robot Romo you will see how Keller Renault used experience as an anchor. To make your message memorable, tie it to a story, an analogy, or an experience.

Visual aids

Many speakers think, "If I use props, slides, or any other visual aids my speech will become more effective." That's wrong. Sometimes visual aids may be harmful.

In Tyler's speech the bacterium and the virus were demonstrated with props and pictures on slides. It made the speech more visual and effective because it's quite difficult for the audience to imagine a bacterium or a virus.

Imagine that the speaker tells a tale about a hare and tortoise. After the premise introduction he shows a stuffed hare and tortoise as a demonstration of the characters in a story. Then you see slides where a conversation between the hare and tortoise is depicted. You may think, "Come on, I know how the hare and the tortoise look. These props… slides… It's silly."

If you doubt whether to use props, videos, slides, or demonstrations in a speech ask yourself, "If I were the audience member would this visual aid make my experience better?"

Remember that everything you do on stage has its purpose. When you gesture, it's not because you don't know what to do with your hands, but to make a speech more visual. When you walk on stage, it's not because you need to warm up the legs, but to make a speech more visual. When you use the props or slides, it's because in this particular situation they make a story more captivating.

Energy on stage

Is Tyler passionate about the topic of his speech? Absolutely! Does Tyler believe that teaching science to students through stories is effective? Absolutely! Energy on stage is contagious and if a speaker is passionate about his or her topic an audience becomes excited to hear a speech.

Make sure that you are always excited to share your message with the audience and your speech will certainly be successful.

Contrast

In terms of good use of contrast, this speech is an excellent example because Tyler broke all kinds of patterns imaginable. Tyler spoke at a fast pace, at a low pace, occasionally paused, and sometimes didn't speak at all. Tyler spoke loudly and silently. Tyler gestured with two hands symmetrically, asymmetrically, with one hand only, and sometimes kept his hands in the resting position.

Supporting materials used for the speech were also varied. Tyler used PowerPoint, props, live demonstration of explosions, and sometimes spoke without any supporting visual aids.

Watch the speech again and notice how the patterns are constantly broken in Tyler's speech. When you use contrast there may be listeners who will accept your message and listeners who won't. However, you can be sure that the attention of all of them will be yours completely. Why? It's very difficult to be distracted from a speaker if everything in his delivery changes all the time.

Use of gestures

Firstly, there was a great variety of gestures during the speech. There were gestures made with one hand, symmetric gestures, asymmetric gestures, and occasionally no gestures at all. Such variety adds contrast to the speech and helps to keep the audience engaged. When gestures are monotonous and repetitive, the audience may get bored and be easily distracted.

Secondly, all gestures in Tyler's speech had meaning and helped to make stories more visual. Often speakers make certain gestures simply because they feel nervous or uncomfortable. For example, a speaker can rub his nose, play with his hair or put a hand in a pocket. These gestures irritate the audience, don't convey any information, and break rapport with the audience. Avoid them by all means.

To improve:

What happened with Tyler's hands when he finished a gesture? The hands moved to a resting position where they either hung in the air with elbows bent at 90 degrees, or the fingers of both hands were put together to form a little pyramid.

As we already discussed, there is only one effective and natural resting position for the hands where they are hanging fully relaxed along the body. Imagine that a speaker, instead of being silent during pauses, hisses. Producing noise during pauses is as irritating for the ear as it is irritating for the eye when the hands do not return to the natural resting position. Tyler's speech will be improved if his hands are "silent" between gestures and hang fully relaxed along the body.

The speech, "Hey, science teachers – make it fun!" can also benefit from broader gestures. How can Tyler make gestures broader? By straightening the hand during each gesture and keeping the elbow further from the body. Broad gestures convey confidence and trustworthiness of the speaker.

Overall gestures were done excellently and helped to illustrate the content. Changing the resting position and making broader gestures can make the speech even more effective.

Eye contact

If you observe how Tyler maintained eye contact with the audience, you will notice that occasionally he looked either at the floor or to the side.

Every time you take the eyes away from the audience, it breaks connection a little. If you don't look at the audience most of the time, there is no way that people will feel engaged and connected with you.

What to do with the eyes when you are on stage? Scan the audience for a couple of seconds and pick one person. Look this person directly in the eye for 5-20 seconds while you finish the idea and then scan the audience to find a new person.

Next time if Tyler avoids taking his eyes away from the audience, the connection with the listeners will be deepened. The audience has an amazing quality that people experience your speech through what happens with a single individual in the room. If you hug one person – everybody feels hugged, if you invite one person on stage – everybody feels engaged, or if you look one person in the eye – everybody feels as you are talking directly to him or her.

Dialogue

What made Tyler's speech particularly engaging was the excellent use of dialogue. For example, dialogue between characters allowed audience members to see action in a story happening right in front of them:

"I came to the classroom and asked, 'Can somebody explain the main ideas and why it is so cool?'"

"'We had to get up in the middle of the night and drive 100 miles in the total darkness.' 'Actually it was 87.3 miles.' And you are like, 'Actually, shut up! I am just trying to tell a story.'"

Besides dialogue between characters, Tyler also has put some of his own thoughts and thoughts of viruses in the form of dialogue:

"If you are a virus you cross your little legs and think, 'We rock!'"

"I am clueless. I have no idea, so the only thing I can think of is, 'Listen. Let me tell you a story!'"

Dialogue breathes life into a speech and turns a boring narration into an exciting experience. There are two rules on how you can make a speech captivating and ensure that it includes enough dialogue.

Firstly, always deliver a character's lines in the form of dialogue. Instead of saying, "When I came home my mom said that I was late," always say, "When I came home my mom said, 'You are late!'"

Secondly, say your own thoughts, thoughts of the audience members, and thoughts of other characters in the form of dialogue. Instead of "I thought that John would definitely win," say, "I thought, 'John will definitely win.'" Instead of "John thought that he would win," say, "John thought, 'I will win.'" Instead of "You probably think that winning is not that difficult," say, "You probably think, 'Winning is not that difficult!'"

In each speech make sure to apply these 2 rules. Every line of dialogue naturally used makes a speech more engaging and hence more successful.

If Tyler asked, "Could you suggest what can make my speech even more effective?" you might say:

Instead of "I am coming to the realization that my students might not be learning anything," say, "I realized, 'My students might not be learning anything!'"

Instead of "And I realized that maybe all my students are in the same boat," say, "And I realized, 'Maybe all my students are in the same boat.'"

Instead of "I was told to never use stories," say, "I was told, 'Tyler, never use stories.'"

If you follow these 2 rules, your audience will feel engaged and excited to hear the speech because they will see a story unfold right in front of their eyes.

Emotional reactions

When you deliver a dialogue line of a character, you also need to convey his or her emotion. Nonverbal reactions are much more eloquent than words and if conveyed properly can make a speech more memorable, engaging, and effective. Tyler not only allowed you to hear what a character said, but also showed what a character felt. For example:

"My favorite student said, 'The reading sucked!'" *(Emotion of surprise. Tyler was very surprised to hear this opinion from his favorite student)*

"Then she clarified, 'I didn't mean it sucked. I did mean that I didn't understand a word of it. It's boring. And who cares?'" *(Again reaction of surprise)*

"And you are just like, 'Oh, my God. What is the point?'" *(Angriness and irritation)*

"And you are like, 'Actually, shut up! I am just trying to tell a story.'" *(Emotion of anger and irritation)*

Emotional reactions are one of those things that differentiate a world-class speech from a good one.

Never hide

If Tyler asked, "Andrii, what change in delivery could significantly improve my speech and is very easy to implement?" I would certainly say, "Don't hide behind the table during the speech. When you speak and the audience sees only half of you, they receive only half of the information from your body language. Besides that, a speaker who hides behind a table or a lectern is perceived as insincere. Either speak in front of the table or remove the table from the stage. The additional value that the demonstration of chemical reactions provides is much less than the harm that speaking behind the table does."

Remember that it's your responsibility as a speaker to make sure that the audience members can see your entire body.

Speech 3: Keller Rinaudo: A mini robot – powered by your phone

Access this and other videos used in this book here: https://andriisedniev.com/magicofspeechevaluation

Use of stories

As you remember to make a point memorable, you need to associate it with a visual anchor: a story, an analogy, or an experience. This speech is an example where experience is used as an anchor.

Imagine a girl who came home after hearing Keller's speech. She might say, "Mom, Mom, I saw a real robot today. It can move, smile, and even play hide and seek!" A girl will remember this speech for a long time because it is tied to the story that happened in her own life. If you want your point to be remembered, you can associate it with a story from your life. However, you can also create an experience for the audience members that will become a story from their life.

Do you remember a story that Keller told about a girl and her grandma who played hide and seek while being in different geographic locations? This story is less than 20 seconds long, and it's not the most impressive story in the world; however, it vividly illustrates an example of how the robot can be used remotely. A story that you use to illustrate a point shouldn't necessarily be remarkable or long. Even a mediocre story, analogy, or experience can make your speech world-class. Why? Because it will be remembered and hence have impact on the lives of the audience members.

3 foundations of public speaking

Did Keller use stories, analogies, or experience to illustrate his point? Yes. Was Keller excited and passionate about the topic of his speech? Yes. Did Keller speak sincerely? Yes.

If the answer is "yes" on these 3 questions, you can be sure that the speech will be perceived well by the audience. Use of stories, sincerity, and energy are the 3 foundations of public speaking and often determine effectiveness of the speech. Why? Because they impact the quality of your speech more than all other techniques combined.

The speech "A mini robot – powered by your phone" is an excellent example of how the proper use of the 3 foundations of public speaking can make a speech effective. When you evaluate speeches of other speakers or work on your own, always first check if sincerity, energy, and stories are there.

Always talk to one person

Imagine that you sit in the audience and hear a speaker saying, "How many of you have a robot at home?" How would you feel? You might think, "I am treated as a part of a large group. The speaker doesn't see an individual in me." What if a speaker instead said, "Do you have a robot at home?" You may think, "I feel like the speaker is talking directly to me. He treats me as an individual."

If you want to connect with the audience, always talk to one person. Every time you say "many of you," "majority of you," or "some of you," the connection with the audience weakens a little. Every time you say "you," a connection deepens a little. If you address the audience many times during the speech, the way you treat each individual may have a significant impact on the effectiveness of the speech.

How can the speech "A mini robot – powered by your phone" become more effective by applying this rule?

Instead of "By show of hands, how many of you have a robot at home?" say, "Raise your hand if you have a robot at home."

Instead of "If any of you guys had this app on your phone…" say, "If you had this app on your phone…"

If every audience member feels that you speak directly to him or her, they will listen more attentively and accept your messages in the end. Remember, no matter how many people sit in the room, always talk to one person.

Audience engagement

Keller excellently engaged the audience members and turned them into the active participants of the speech rather than observers. How did he do that?

Firstly, at the beginning of the speech Keller asked the audience members to raise a hand if they have a robot at home. Requesting to raise a hand is perhaps one of the most common ways to engage the audience.

People usually expect a speech to be a lecture where they don't participate, and prepare to be observers. Even the smallest engagement may have a significant impact on the attitude of the audience members to the speech. If you engage the audience during the first few minutes they realize, "Hey, it's not the usual lecture. Maybe this speech will be an interesting experience where I am an active participant. I will listen to this speaker."

After you have engaged the audience members with something small, like raising a hand, you can ask them later during the speech to do something more significant like driving a robot, repeating a phrase, or even dancing.

Secondly, Keller asked for a volunteer from the audience to drive a robot and once a man volunteered said, "Thanks, Scott." It helped Keller to connect with the audience. But why?

An audience has an amazing quality in that all the people experience your speech through one person. If you call one person by name, everybody feels like they were called by name. If you let one person drive a robot, everybody feels like they have participated. Keller gave Scott control over the robot, called him by name, and everybody in the audience felt like a star.

If the audience members are engaged, you connect with them. If audience members are engaged, they listen more attentively. If audience members are engaged, they feel like co-authors of the speech and believe in your messages as in their own.

After watching this speech, remember these 2 tips for audience engagement: Engage the audience by asking them to do something small within the first few minutes of the speech, and make the entire audience feel like a star by engaging one person.

Connect unfamiliar information with what the audience already knows

Remember when Keller said, "Romo can stream two-way audio and video between any two smart devices"? In any technical presentation, when you say a phrase like this it is often not only difficult for the audience to remember but also to understand.

If you want unfamiliar information to be remembered, illustrate it with an analogy or story based on information that the audience already knows.

Keller did it greatly by using the analogy, "It's like Skype on wheels," and then telling a short story, "Imagine an 8-year-old girl… "

The audience may find it far easier to imagine a girl playing hide and seek with her grandmother or "Skype on wheels" than "two-way stream of audio and video between smart devices."

How we can apply this rule to make the speech "A mini robot powered by your phone" even more effective?

"Blockly allows you to drag and drop blocks of semantic code to create a behavior for Romo. You can also download some behavior for the robot created by another user."

This information will more likely be remembered if it is illustrated with an example such as, "Using a simple interface you can make Romo dance in a funny way, and upload the video on YouTube. If your friends like the dance, they can download this behavior and make their robots dance in exactly the same way."

It doesn't matter if your story or analogy is short, long, fictional, or mediocre. Any story will make the audience understand technical information better. Why? A story or analogy connects unfamiliar information with what the audience members already know and this connection makes unfamiliar information easy to remember.

Gestures

Keller's gestures were broad and versatile. All gestures were meaningful and helped to illustrate a message. One thing that could make them even more effective is a natural resting position. If Keller returns his hands to the natural resting position, it will give gestures greater amplitude and make them more meaningful. Remember? A natural resting position is when hands are hanging relaxed along the body. Pause not only with your voice but also with your body.

Speech 4: Lewis Pugh swims the North Pole

Access this and other videos used in this book here: https://andriisedniev.com/magicofspeechevaluation

Promote a process

Whether you have won an Olympic gold medal in swimming or climbed Mt. Everest, never brag about the achievement itself. Instead, promote a process that allowed you to get from where you were before to where you are now.

If you brag about your achievement, the audience members will think, "Hey, this guy is too narcissistic. When I hear about all his achievements, I feel bad about myself" or "This speaker is talented. This speaker is lucky. This speaker is special. Of course he could achieve this, but I, ordinary John, will never be able to."

Show the audience members that you are similar to them. It was the process that allowed you to get from where you were before to where you are now and if the audience uses it they too will be able to achieve the same.

Lewis Pugh is aware of how dangerous his endeavor was and focuses not on the achievement itself but on what made it possible: a professional team of 27 people, mental preparation, a 5-minute trial swim, and support of his friend.

It may be unlikely that you will ever want to swim at the North Pole. However, if you wanted to do it, after Lewis's speech you know the process that will allow you to achieve this goal. Remember that achievement can't change anyone's life but the process can.

Be succinct

The main goal of the speech is to make the audience remember your points. If you share only the information that is necessary to support your message, it will have a better chance of being remembered.

If you share information that is very interesting, but not essential for supporting the point, it will actually make your messages less memorable and the speech less effective.

Lewis's speech will highly benefit if the redundant information is thrown away. You might think, "How can I determine which information to leave out?" It's very easy. Ask yourself, "Would the speech become less valuable if this particular fact or sentence wasn't there?" If the answer is no, then leaving it out will make the speech stronger.

For example:

"Today I want to talk to you about swimming across the North Pole, across the most northern place in the whole world." *(Just talk about swimming at the North Pole. Don't waste precious stage time by saying that you want to talk about it.)*

"My father was a great storyteller. He could tell a story about an event and you felt absolutely there at the moment." *(The fact that Lewis's father was a great storyteller isn't important for the speech. When you speak on stage all the information you share should be necessary to support a point. Your goal is to change people's lives for the better, not to share with them your biography.)*

"Sorry, but there is no other way to describe it." *(Apology never adds value to the speech. No matter what you said, just continue.)*

"I just wanted to end by saying this." *(Just say it. Don't say that you want to say it.)*

If by cutting unnecessary sentences you turn a 10-minute speech into an 8.5-minute speech, then it will become significantly more effective.

Dialogue

Dialogue allows the audience to see how a story develops right in front of their eyes instead of hearing narration about what happened in the past. Lewis did use dialogue and it helped to make his speech interesting and engaging. For example:

"I had my coach screaming for me: 'Come on, Lewis, go, go. Don't slow down.'"

"At a local hospital they said, 'Ran, there is no possibility of us being able to save these fingers.'"

"And my close friend David said, 'Lewis, I have known you since you were 18 years old. I know, Lewis, that you are going to make this swim.'"

If Lewis applied the 2 dialogue rules we discussed earlier, it would increase the concentration of dialogue and make the story even more alive for the audience.

Remember what the rules said? "Always tell characters' lines in dialogue. Always say your thoughts, thoughts of the audience members, and thoughts of the characters in dialogue."

Instead of "He said that the explosion was so light and the explosion was so intense that…" say, "He said, 'The explosion was so light and the explosion was so intense that…'"

Instead of "So I decided to do this symbolic swim," say, "So I decided, 'I will do this symbolic swim.'"

Instead of "On day 4 we decided to do a quick 5-minute test swim," say, "On day 4 we decided, 'Let's do a quick 5-minute test swim and see how it goes.'"

When you say the same piece of information in a form of dialogue, it may have a significant positive impact on the effectiveness of the speech. Remember the 2 rules of dialogue and I am sure your speeches will always be engaging and interesting.

Perfect story structure

Lewis used a perfect story structure in his speech. It made audience members curious about development of the story and so touched, that they even gave Lewis standing ovations in the end.

Premise introduction

Place: The story happens in the sea at the North Pole.

People: Lewis and 27 other members of the team.

Conflict

Lewis wants to make a symbolic swim to draw the attention of politicians in the entire world to the problem of climate change at the North Pole. It was extremely difficult to do because swimming in water at such low temperatures is dangerous.

Conflict escalation

After a 5-minute test swim Lewis couldn't feel his fingers. Lewis thought that he could fail to fulfill his dream and lose his fingers.

Climax

In the climax scene Lewis showed a video of his swim and let the audience see how the conflict got resolved.

Always ask yourself, "How can I make my story adhere even more to the perfect story structure," and your audiences will be looking forward to each of your speeches.

Leave no questions unanswered

Your speech constantly creates and answers questions in the minds of the audience members. For example, they may think "What will happen with the character next?" "Why should I care about the climate change?" or "How can I benefit from this insight?"

Have you ever watched an interesting movie that ended abruptly without giving answers to all of your questions? By the end of the speech, all the questions that your story created should be answered or the listeners will feel cheated.

There were several questions that Lewis didn't answer by the end of the speech. "Did your swim actually draw the attention of at least one politician? Did the swim have an impact that made it worth it?" and "What allowed you to not have severe consequences for your health? How did you recover your fingers?"

Even if the audience members enjoyed a story, after leaving the room with questions unanswered they may feel dissatisfied.

If Lewis addresses these questions, it will make the speech stronger. Taking into account the time freed up after making a speech more succinct, these answers won't even prolong the speech.

When you craft a speech think, "What questions would I have if I were the audience member?" and make sure that all questions that your story creates are answered by the end of the speech.

Gestures

Open gestures show that a speaker is sincere and doesn't have anything to hide. Lewis gestured with open hands and it helped to build a connection with the audience. Two changes could make his gestures even more effective.

Firstly, if Lewis makes broader gestures they will be more meaningful and will make him look more confident. You might think, "Andrii, how can I know that the gestures are broad?" It's very easy. When a gesture is broad there is a distance between the elbow and the body, and the angle at the elbow is more than 90 degrees.

Secondly, after the end of the gesture, Lewis put his fingers together forming a pyramid, which made his resting position distracting and gestures not as effective as they could be. Returning hands to the natural resting position (hands hanging relaxed along the body) can add more amplitude and meaning to the gestures.

3 foundations of public speaking

Lewis did tell stories in his speech, he was passionate about the topic, and he was sincere. When a speech includes the 3 foundations of public speaking it is always strong. In Lewis's case it even got a standing ovation.

Summary phrase

The purpose of the story is to support a takeaway message that a speaker wants the audience to remember. If you were to summarize the entire speech into one sentence, it would be a summary phrase.

Lewis finished his speech with a summary phrase, "We must all ask ourselves what kind of decisions we are going to make today to ensure that we live in a sustainable world." People remember best what they hear last and for the speech to have an impact on the audience, it is very effective to repeat a summary phrase in conclusion.

Following 3 rules of the summary phrase will make Lewis's speech even more focused and powerful.

Rule 1: Talk to one person

The summary phrase should always be focused on one person. Instead of "We must all ask ourselves a question…" say, "Ask yourself a question…" If you address your message to one person, everybody in the audience will feel that you are talking directly to him or her and will much more likely take action.

If you say, "This problem affects all of us. Everybody needs to take action," people will think, "Hey, somebody else will take care of it. I'll just wait and do nothing."

But if you say, "This problem affects you. Take action today," people will think, "Hey, this problem is relevant to me. The speaker talks to me personally. I might do something about it."

Remember that you should always address the entire audience as one person in a summary phrase.

Rule 2: Be specific

If you say, "We must all ask ourselves what kind of decisions we are going to make today to ensure that we live in a sustainable world," the audience members may be confused about what exactly they should do. They might think, "What do you mean by sustainable world? How can I benefit from asking myself a question? OK, I see that the climate is changing, but why is it dangerous to me personally and what exactly do you suggest I do about it?"

If you want an audience member to do something differently after the speech, the summary phrase should be as clear and actionable as possible.

For example, imagine that by the end of the speech a speaker says, "If you want to live longer you need to have a healthy lifestyle." Everybody will get confused because it's not clear what a "healthy lifestyle" is, and how to implement the recommendation. People will never do what they don't understand.

However if a speaker says, "Jog every day for 30 minutes and you will live 10 years longer than your friends who don't," some audience members will follow the advice because they will understand exactly how to implement the recommendation.

Rule 3: Speech should be built around a summary phrase

When you create a speech, decide first what the summary phrase is and only then decide which stories, facts, or statistics are necessary to support it. If a story or a fact doesn't help to support a summary phrase – leave it out no matter how interesting it is.

If you want to change the lives of the audience members and make them take your advice seriously, a speech should be laser focused on the summary phrase. Otherwise the power of your message will be diluted.

Lewis's speech about a swim at the North Pole would become more focused and powerful if information that is not critical to support a summary phrase were eliminated. For example, the fact that Lewis's father was an excellent story teller is not necessary to support the takeaway message.

Speech 5: Ray Zahab treks to the South Pole

Access this and other videos used in this book here: https://andriisedniev.com/magicofspeechevaluation

3 foundations of public speaking

Energy

If a speaker is passionate about his or her topic, the audience will become passionate about it as well.

Ray is extremely passionate about his trip to the South Pole and his energy is contagious. "Ray Zahab treks to the South Pole" is an excellent example of the positive impact that being energetic can have on captivating the audience.

Story

Ray went through an extremely interesting adventure. However, his speech would become more memorable if it included a story. How could Ray turn a narration about trekking to the South Pole into a story?

By adding elements that make a story a story: conflict, escalation of the conflict, climax scene, dialogue between characters, and actions. People remember facts only when they are tied to stories, analogies, or experiences.

Use of visual aids

Ray used visual aids effectively. The photographs on the slides and a short video helped to make the speech more visual for the audience members. PowerPoint is for pictures, graphs, and diagrams, not for words. People can't simultaneously read and listen to you and if you have more than 8 words on the slide either you or PowerPoint is redundant.

Remember, if you decide to use a slide to supplement a speech, use it to demonstrate photos, graphs, diagrams, or videos and not the text.

Exact numbers

In his speech Ray said, "Together we had just broken the world speed record for a trek to the South Pole. It took us 33 days, 23 hours, and 55 minutes to get there." Ray could have said that it took them 34 days to get to the South Pole, but instead he gave the exact number. Why?

Firstly, exact numbers make a story more believable. If you remember the exact duration of your trip to the South Pole then there is no doubt that you have been there.

Secondly, exact numbers convey more information than rounded numbers. "33 days, 23 hours, and 55 minutes" tells the audience that the trip was very important for Ray (he remembered the duration). It also tells that the time was measured because the team aimed to break the world record.

When it is important for a story, don't round the numbers. Exact numbers convey more information and sometimes make a story funnier.

Leave no questions unanswered

If Ray answered the questions that his speech created: "Why did you go to the South Pole?" "How did you prepare for this trip to make it possible?" "How can I benefit from your expericnce?" and, finally, "How did you go to the bathroom at such low temperatures?" it would help to avoid upsetting the listeners.

If you don't answer all questions that popped up in the minds of the audience members during the speech, they may feel cheated and unsatisfied even if your speech was great overall.

Promote a process

Imagine that you are the audience member and hear a speaker telling a story, "I became the first person in history to make an entire 650-mile journey from Hercules Inlet to the South Pole without skis. Such a trip is extremely dangerous for ordinary people because of extreme temperatures, long distance, and huge cracks in the ice. But guess what? I did it and didn't even encounter major difficulties on the way. Two years ago I also made a 111-day run across the Sahara desert. And by the way, I managed to accomplish all these only after 5 years of running. Before that I was a smoker and didn't exercise."

Imagine if the same speaker tells this story in the following way, "I am not any better or more talented than you. The trip to the South Pole has been successful not because I was lucky or talented, but because of the process I used. Here is how we prepared... Here is the process that was used... Here are the lessons we learned along the way. If you use the same process, you might achieve the same as I did if not more. I highly encourage you to use this process and I am really eager to see you succeed in achieving your goals."

Do you see the difference? In the first story a speaker is bragging about himself and in the second he promotes a process. In the first he makes the audience members envy him and in the second he inspires them and gives value. In the first he shows that he is special and in the second he connects with the audience. Just a slight change of focus in a story may have enormous impact on its effectiveness.

If Ray changes the focus in his speech to promoting a process and giving insights to the audience members that can change their lives for the better, it will make his speech more valuable and memorable. Audience members don't care about your life. They care about how they can apply lessons from your experience to change their lives for the better.

Movements on stage

Movements on stage should visually illustrate a speech and have a purpose. There are 3 major reasons why you may decide to move on stage.

Firstly, when you finish telling one story and move to another. In this case, two spots on stage are associated with different stories. When you return to one of these spots listeners will remember a story you told standing there.

Secondly, you can move from left to right *(from the audience's perspective)* when events in a story happened at different times. For example you can tell a story about a run in the Sahara desert, then move a couple of steps to the left and tell a story about a trip to the South Pole, then move a couple of steps left again and tell about what happened with you today. In this case, each spot on stage represents different points in time. At the end of the speech, you can refer to these spots. The audience members will recall events that happened at each of the spots.

Finally, you can walk to a different spot when movement on stage replicates action in a story. For example, you may say, "I exited the office. Walked a couple of blocks to the nearby cafe" and simultaneously move to a new spot on stage. The spot you left represents the office and the spot you moved to represents the cafe.

If Ray stands still or moves with a purpose, he will hold the attention of the audience even better. Walking on stage without purpose distracts an audience and makes your message less memorable.

Gestures

If Ray avoids keeping his left hand in his pocket, his gestures will become more effective because of 2 reasons.

Firstly, Ray will be able to gesture with two hands instead of one and add variety to the gestures. Using 2 hands for gestures makes a speech more visual.

Secondly, a hand in the pocket draws the attention of the audience members and makes them think about the hand instead of the speech.

Speech 6: Ric Elias: 3 things I learned while my plane crashed

Access this and other videos used in this book here: https://andriisedniev.com/magicofspeechevaluation

Rule of 3

"Imagine a big explosion. Imagine a plane full of smoke. Imagine the engine going clank, clank, clank…" Ric Elias used the rule of 3 excellently in the beginning of the speech.

Letting the audience imagine 3 things rather than 2 or 4 immerses them into the story better. Why? The number 3 has incredible impact on our brain.

Firstly, hearing information in a quantity of 3 is pleasant for the ear. Secondly, when you say 3 examples, 3 characteristics, or 3 arguments, people remember them better. Look where you can naturally apply the rule of 3 in a speech to make it more effective.

Imagine

The word "imagine" has a magic impact on the audience. It engages imagination and puts audience members right in the middle of the action. The word "imagine" activates the senses of the listeners and makes a story much more visual, tangible, and memorable. Ric began his speech with, "Imagine a big explosion. Imagine a plane full of smoke…" and it allowed him to captivate the attention of the audience members and to put them mentally in the middle of the scene in the story.

Gestures

Ric used an effective resting position for his hands. When his hands weren't gesturing, they were hanging relaxed along the body. This resting position doesn't distract the audience, conveys confidence of the speaker, and gives gestures bigger amplitude.

The gestures were versatile and meaningful. For example, Ric gestured with 2 hands, with one hand, and sometimes didn't gesture. This allowed him to avoid patterns in delivery and to keep the audience engaged.

If Ric uses broader gestures, he will look even more confident and his body language will be even more meaningful. What is a broad gesture? A gesture is broad if there is a distance between an elbow and the body and the angle at the elbow is more than 90 degrees.

Movements

Ric told one short story about the plane crash in which he was sitting during an entire flight. Remember 3 reasons to walk on stage? There was no reason for Ric to walk on stage and he didn't. This helped to avoid distracting the audience and to concentrate the attention of the listeners on the speaker.

Ric will be able to hold the attention of the audience focused on his message even better if he doesn't dance from one leg to another. *(Shifting weight from one leg to another)*

Sometimes speakers make irrelevant movements or gestures on stage without even knowing that they do them. Dancing from one leg to another, touching the nose, playing with hair, or rubbing a finger may distract the attention of the audience and even diminish the authority of the speaker.

The good news is that it is very easy to get rid of such movements. Once you watch your speech on video and notice irrelevant movements or gestures, you may think, "I never thought I was doing this. It looks awkward. Next time I will make sure to not do it again." After several speeches, you will not have to control if you are doing irrelevant movement or not because this habit will be gone.

Be specific

Ric's speech will become much more visual, tangible, and clear if he avoids using complex terms and ambiguous language. For example: "I had a good life." "Good life" is a complex term, because everybody understands it differently. You might think, "Good life is when you have a wife, kids, and several friends." Your audience member may think, "Good life is when you make a lot of money and are successful in your career" or "Good life is when you have good health and have enough money for food." If you use a complex term, always clarify what it means for you to be on the same page with the audience.

"I tried to get better at everything I've tried." "Everything I have tried" is ambiguous for the audience. The audience doesn't know what "everything" means. The audience doesn't know exactly what you have tried. If the audience doesn't understand what you are talking about, they will not remember your message.

Always ask yourself, "Would a 10-year-old kid understand clearly what I say?" If your answer is "yes" then the speech is clear and specific enough for any audience. Your information is very likely to be understood and remembered.

Use simple words, explain difficult concepts, and give visual examples. The value of your speech lies in specifics.

3 foundations of public speaking

Sincerity

Ric's delivery was sincere. You could sense that he genuinely wanted the audience members to rethink what is important in life.

Energy

Ric told a story about a plane crash like it was an article from the newspaper, rather than an event from his life. Ric's speech would have more impact if he relived the story on stage and was emotionally engaged.

The more time has passed after a major event, the less emotional you become about it. However, on stage you should tell a story with such emotions, as if it is happening right now in front of the audience.

You might think, "Andrii, how can I feel again emotions that I felt many years ago? Is it at all possible?"

Actually, it is not difficult to do. Close your eyes and imagine a story that happened to you. Remember as vividly as possible what you heard, saw, thought, and felt. After several minutes, you will be able to feel the same emotions as in the event that happened several years ago. Watching videos and photos from the past also helps significantly to recall memories. Once you get fully immersed in the atmosphere of the story, practice telling it at home several times.

On the day of the presentation, you will be able to feel the emotions that you felt in the past on stage and make the audience relive a story with you. I call this technique "emotional storytelling."

Story

Ric's speech is an excellent example that even an incomplete story can have significant positive impact on how the message is remembered. The story about the airplane crash doesn't have a climax, and doesn't have dialogue among characters, but I can remember it even weeks after hearing it from Ric.

Of course, a story that adheres to the perfect story structure is more effective than a story that doesn't. However, the fact that you do use a story has much bigger impact on effectiveness of a speech than the quality of the story. A beginner speaker who tells a story is always more effective on stage than an experienced speaker with perfect delivery who doesn't.

1 point per 10 minutes

If you try to make 2, 3 or more points during 10 minutes of a speech, most probably none of them will be remembered. Why? Even if you tie a point to a story, there will be too little time to make it stick. Aim to deliver on average 1 point per 10 minutes. If your speech lasts 60 minutes, for example, you can't make more than 6 points.

Ric's speech lasted 5 minutes and had 3 takeaway messages. The story lasted 1.5 minutes and 3 points lasted 3.5 minutes. The speech can't make a lasting positive impact on the audience if it isn't remembered.

If Ric asked, "Andrii, can you give one piece of advice that could make my speech more effective?" I would say, "You see, Ric, for the speech that lasts 5 minutes you have a choice. Either make 3 points, none of which the audience will remember, or make just one point that the audience may remember for years. If you want to change the lives of the audience members, reduce the number of points to one and use the freed time to expand the story."

Speech 7: Ron Finley: A guerrilla gardener in South Central LA

Access this and other videos used in this book here: https://andriisedniev.com/magicofspeechevaluation

3 foundations of public speaking

Ron does use short stories that help to make his messages memorable. Two examples are a story about the warning he received from the city council and a story about a mother and a daughter looking at Ron's garden.

Ron also uses analogies effectively to make his points more visual. "I see wheelchairs bought and sold like used cars" is more visual than "I see that wheelchairs are bought and sold often." "Growing your own food is like printing your own money" is more visual than "Growing your own food is profitable."

Ron sincerely believes that gardening in the city can make the lives of the audience members better. Ron is extremely passionate about his topic and it is contagious. If you asked me, "Andrii, could you point out a speech where I could clearly see what being energetic and passionate on stage means?" Ron's speech would be certainly one of those I would point at.

If you are sincere, energetic, and use stories, your speech will be strong. Why? Because these 3 public speaking techniques have more impact on your success than all others.

However, if you don't implement at least 2 of these 3 fundamental techniques, it may be very difficult if not impossible to make your message accepted and remembered.

Dialogue

Ron used dialogue in his speech, excellently. For example:

Thoughts in a form of dialogue:

"So I am like, 'Cool, I'll do whatever the hell I want.'"

"I'm like, 'Come on. Really? A warning about a piece of land that you couldn't care less about?'"

Characters' lines in a form of dialogue:

"Friends are asking, 'Hey, Ron, aren't you afraid that people are going to steal your food?'"

"No, I am not afraid they are going to steal it. That's why it is on the street. That's the whole idea."

A dialogue turns a dry narration into an action movie. Dialogue places audience members in the middle of the scene. Instead of just hearing about a story, dialogue allows the audience members to see action develop in front of their eyes.

Body language

Excellent:

Ron's hands return to the natural resting position when he is not gesturing. This gives gestures more amplitude and meaning. Gestures are also very versatile. Ron gestures with one hand, with 2 hands, and sometimes doesn't gesture at all.

To improve:

Everything you do on stage should have meaning. Otherwise irrelevant movements or gestures can distract audience members from the speech. For example, every time you rub your nose, the attention of the audience may be focused on the nose instead of the speech.

Ron will hold the attention of the audience members even better if he eliminates purposeless movements on stage, rubbing his nose, and putting a hand in his pocket.

Contrast

Ron speaks quickly, slowly, and sometimes makes pauses. Ron changes the volume of his speech and makes different gestures. He also interchanges stories with analogies.

When everything a speaker does on stage changes, the brains of the audience members can't find a pattern. If audience members don't see patterns in delivery, their attention is fully concentrated on a speech. No matter what the speech is about, if everything the speaker does changes, it is very difficult to not be attentive.

Use of PowerPoint

Slides were used very effectively. Photos helped the audience to visualize the speech better. When text was used, there were no more than 8 words on a slide.

Remember that people can't simultaneously read and listen to a speaker? If there are significantly more than 8 words on a slide, the audience will be focused fully on the slide while reading the text and won't be paying attention to you.

Interchange a story with a conversation

Do you remember a speaker who told his or her entire speech like this: "I began learning to swim at the age of 9. I became a professional athlete when I was 14. My coach taught me to be purposeful. In the summer I flew to Berlin to participate in a competition…" and only in the last sentence remembered the audience, "If you want to succeed – be purposeful."

Do you see a problem here? When a speaker talks all the time in monologue, you feel disengaged and quickly get bored. If you want audience members to be engaged and attentive, always speak in a form of conversation. Ron did it excellently with such phrases as:

"It's owned by the city but YOU have to maintain it."

"Growing one plant will give YOU 10,000 seeds."

"YOU'LL be surprised what soil could do if you let it be YOUR canvas."

"YOU'LL be surprised how kids are affected by this."

"Gardening is the most therapeutic act YOU can do."

"If YOU want to meet with me…"

When you address audience members or ask them a question, it turns a monologue into a conversation. Do you see what is common among the phrases mentioned above? They all have the word "YOU." Make sure that your speech has the word "YOU" not only at the end of the speech but also in the middle. When you have a conversation with the audience members they listen more attentively, enjoy a speech more, and accept your messages more likely.

Eye contact

Choose one audience member, look him or her in the eye for 5-20 seconds until you finish a thought, and then randomly choose another audience member for eye contact.

When you look one listener in the eye, the audience feels like you look everybody in the eye. When you take your eyes away from the audience, people feel like you don't look anybody in the eye and it breaks the connection.

Occasionally, Ron looked at the floor or to the side. If Ron looks one person in the eye for a few seconds, scans the room, looks the next person in the eye for a few seconds and then repeats this cycle, his connection with the audience will be even stronger.

Use of statistics

Ron made numbers in his speech visual and meaningful. He said: "A city owns 26 square miles of vacant lots. It's 20 Central Parks." The audience members can't visualize 26 square miles, but can easily visualize 20 Central Parks. The audience can't understand whether 26 square miles is a big area, but can easily understand whether the area equivalent to 20 Central Parks is big or not. Statistics in a speech can have impact on people only if they understand what those numbers mean.

Rule of 3

Ron effectively applied the rule of 3 several times in his speech. For example: "Liquor stores, fast food, vacant lots." Three examples are more effective than 2 or 4. Three examples of what represents South Central are more pleasant for the ear, are easier to remember, and make a picture in the imagination of the audience members more visual.

Pause

Pause is one of the most powerful tools in a speaker's arsenal. Audience members don't change when they hear your words, they change only after they think about them.

Each time you say something important, pause for 1-3 seconds to give audience members an opportunity to think. Even if your speech is extremely valuable and has important points, it may have no impact if your listeners don't have time to think.

Remember that not your words, but the thoughts of the audience members transform their lives. Ron excellently used a pause in his speech and audience members had enough time to think about his words.

Speech 8: Damon Horowitz: Philosophy in prison

Access this and other videos used in this book here: https://andriisedniev.com/magicofspeechevaluation

Energy and Story

Yes, Damon is energetic on stage. When the speaker is energetic and passionate about his message, audience members can't get bored or fall asleep. Why? Because energy is contagious.

Yes, Damon tells a story and it helps to make his message memorable for the audience members. However, for the message to be accepted, audience members should trust a speaker and they trust a speaker only if he or she is genuine.

Genuine

The biggest drawback of the "Philosophy in prison" speech was the insincere delivery. However, this speech is extremely valuable for us to discuss what exactly can make a speech insincere.

Acting is very different from public speaking. When an actor plays a role there is an invisible wall between him and the audience. It means whether people are present in the audience or not, his delivery will not be any different. If Damon talked to the audience in a conversational manner rather than delivered a rehearsed text, it would create a connection and impact the lives of the audience members.

If Damon is himself on stage and doesn't play a role, his delivery will become more genuine. When you speak eloquently, do unnatural gestures, or try to resemble a famous speaker, audience members instantly realize that you are not sincere and are pretending to be somebody you are not.

Being sincere on stage is perhaps the most important thing in public speaking. People will forgive you anything but being insincere. Never try to create a better version of yourself on stage. Speak to the audience just like you do in everyday life. People don't need another Tony Robbins, Socrates or Churchill, they need YOU.

If you want to be sincere and connect with the audience, talk to them as to your best friend. Imagine that your best friend says, "Hi. Our enemy is thoughtlessness" or "What can creatures like us know of such things?" You may think, "Are you nuts? Can you talk to me like a human?" Guess what? If you try to appear clever or eloquent on stage and use language not commonly used in conversations, the audience will think the same.

Language that is appropriate for a novel or a scientific paper may sound terrible on stage. Vocabulary used in conversational language is smaller and sentences are shorter than in written language. No matter what your speech is about, always talk to the audience as to your best friend, using vocabulary and sentences you use in everyday conversations. Audience will realize that you are sincere and will listen attentively to your every word.

Dialogue delivery

Dialogue in Damon's speech allowed audience members to see actions unfold in front of their eyes and made a story engaging. Delivery would be more sincere if Damon didn't parody his student and acted out dialogues naturally.

Imagine a speaker who acts out a dialogue between him and his 5-year-old daughter. He uses her tone of voice, her gestures, and behaves on stage just like her. How does it look? Behaving like a character may look great in a parody show or theatrical play, however in public speech it looks awkward and insincere.

Your audience only needs to know which character is talking at each particular moment. If you change your posture, gestures, or intonation slightly, the audience members will clearly understand which character is talking.

If you talk with your usual voice, and make your usual gestures with a very slight change, you will not only avoid distracting the audience, but also will look sincere. When you talk on behalf of your 5-year-old daughter or a gangster, don't try to imitate their voices or gestures.

Contrast

Damon's speech is very good in terms of contrast and breaking patterns. Even though the speech has issues with sincerity in delivery and connection between the speaker and the audience, it is almost impossible not to be attentive. Damon changes his pace of speaking, tone of voice, volume and gestures; he also interchanges narration with dialogue, moves on stage, and sometimes doesn't move, breaking all possible patterns.

If you change everything you do on stage, patterns aren't formed. Audience members will pay attention to you during the entire speech because it is very difficult not to if everything on stage changes all the time.

Speech 9: Hans Rosling: The magic washing machine

Access this and other videos used in this book here: https://andriisedniev.com/magicofspeechevaluation

Eye contact

If I were to give only one recommendation to Hans about making a speech even more effective, it would be this, "Every time you take your eyes away from the audience to look at the slide, connection with the listeners breaks a little. Audience members won't accept a recommendation from a speaker who they don't trust or connect with.

"While you deliver a speech, always maintain eye contact with the audience. Memorize the sequence of slides and switch between them while looking in the eyes of one of the audience members. I am sure at the end of the speech someone will approach you and say: 'Thanks, Hans. It was one of the best speeches I've recently heard. I felt so engaged … And your use of PowerPoint was absolutely impressive.'"

If you want to become a world-class speaker, you need to do things the majority of others don't. Extra effort in remembering the sequence of slides and rehearsing will pay off dramatically on the day of the presentation.

Story vs. statistics

If you consider whether to use a story or statistics to illustrate a point, always choose a story. A story conveys emotions, and a statistic conveys logic. Emotions make people remember information far better than logic.

Remember that people don't remember facts if they are not tied to a story, an analogy, or an exercise?

A story about a woman in Rio, who washes by hand and dreams about a washing machine, is much more effective than statistics saying that several billion people don't have electricity, but might have it in the near future. However, a story backed up by statistics is the most powerful combination you may find to persuade the audience to change their behavior.

Hans shared statistics about how many people in the world own a washing machine and how many don't. He tied these statistics to a short story: "I can assure you that this woman in the favela in Rio wants a washing machine. She is very happy about her minister of energy, Dilma Rousseff. So happy that she even voted for her to become president."

The speech "The magic washing machine" is an excellent example of how facts, statistics, and scientific findings can be illustrated by stories. Stories make facts not only better understood but also more memorable.

Structure

All successful speeches have different content, but all of them have the same structure: opening, body, and closing. The goal of the opening is to break the preoccupation of the audience, draw attention, and give a hint of what the speech will be about. Hans told a story about his mother's first washing machine and this opening reached all these 3 goals.

To tell a short story is one of the most effective ways to begin a speech. People like hearing interesting stories. Stories always draw attention and break the preoccupation of the audience members. In the majority of boring speeches audience members expect to hear something like, "Hi, my name is John. I work as a manager at XYZ. I am happy to be here…" and if they hear a story instead, they think, "Hey, this speech is unusual. I like stories. This speech is worth listening to. I will pay attention."

Consider your opening and especially the first 30 seconds of the speech as an exam. If you pass it, audience members will decide to listen to you. If not, they will decide that your speech is not worth their attention and this decision will be very difficult to change later.

The closing is perhaps the most important part of the entire speech because people remember best what they hear last. The goal of the closing is to summarize main points, give listeners a takeaway message, and leave them at a high energy level.

Hans finished the speech with a story about the washing machine. People like hearing stories and an effective story leaves them with a positive impression about the entire speech. A story is easy to remember and once audience members are asked what the speech was about, they will certainly retell a story. In conclusion Hans also gave a takeaway message that summarized the entire speech, "Thank you, industrialization, for giving us the chance to read more books."

A summary phrase

If I asked you, "Please summarize in one sentence what the audience should remember after the end of the presentation," your answer will be a summary phrase. For example, in

Hans's speech it was "Industrialization gave us a chance to read more books."

Before you begin creating a speech, decide what your summary phrase is. Then ask yourself, "Does this particular fact, statistic, or story support my summary phrase?" If yes, put it into the speech, if not, leave it out. If you don't build a speech around a summary phrase, it's not focused enough. If a speech isn't focused, audience members will be confused and will not remember your message.

Although Hans's speech is very engaging and interesting, it could become even more effective if it were more focused on a single message and single summary phrase. Currently Hans's conclusion and beginning of the speech are focused around the message, "Washing machines made our lives much more convenient. Now we have more free time thanks to washing machines." The body of the speech is focused on another message, "The energy consumption in the world is growing. We need to use more green energy to avoid climate change."

If Hans used facts, statistics, and stories that support a single takeaway message, the speech would become more focused and memorable. If audience members are not confused, they are much more likely to remember a message and change their behavior after the presentation.

Dialogue

Hans's speech has many characters' lines delivered in a form of dialogue. For example:

"Grandma said, 'No, no, no. Let me. Let me push the button.'"

"Environmentally concerned students say, 'No. Everyone in the world can't have cars and washing machines.'"

"I asked my students, 'How many of you don't have a car?'"

"Mom said, 'Now, Hans, we have loaded the laundry. The machine will do the work.'"

Dialogue makes Hans's speech interesting and engaging. You can feel that a story he tells is happening right in front of you. When I was a student most of my professors said less dialogue lines during the entire year than Hans did within 10 minutes. I think that Hans's students are very lucky to have such an engaging professor with excellent public speaking skills.

Contrast

Hans excellently used contrast to avoid creating patterns in his speech delivery. Hans varied his energy, volume of voice, pace of the speech, and gestures. Hans also varied supporting material for his message. He used stories, statistics, examples, and facts.

If an audience member can't find patterns in delivery, his or her attention will be glued to the speaker during the entire speech. If what happens on stage constantly changes, it is very difficult to not pay attention and to think about something else.

Gestures

If instead of the pocket Hans returns his hand to the natural resting position after finishing a gesture *(hand hanging relaxed along the body),* it will give gestures bigger amplitude and make them even more meaningful.

Title should be interesting

Hans created an intriguing title for his speech. Imagine that you came to a TED conference and could only attend one of the sessions that were running simultaneously: "Growth of energy consumption in the world," "Impact of technology on modern society," or "The magic washing machine." Which of these titles makes you more curious?

Spend enough time on creating a title for your speech. If it intrigues audience members, they will be eager to hear your speech even before you say the first word. An interesting title will make your job easier on stage in captivating the audience.

Speech 10: Phil Hansen: Embrace the shake

Access this and other videos used in this book here: https://andriisedniev.com/magicofspeechevaluation

3 foundations of public speaking

Phil Hansen speaks sincerely, and through nonverbal signals you can notice that he relives moments from the past on stage. Phil was very passionate to share his ideas about art and life with the audience, and this energy was contagious.

Finally, Phil began his speech with a story about what led him to create so many unconventional art pieces and turn his limitation into new opportunities.

Although the 3 foundations of public speaking have enormous impact on the success of a speech and are very easy to implement, unfortunately few speakers use all 3 of them.

Let's see what else was done well and what could make the "Embrace the shake" speech even more effective.

Gestures

Phil returned hands to the natural resting position after the end of each gesture. It helped to avoid distracting the audience and gave gestures bigger amplitude.

Broader gestures would make Phil appear even more confident and his body language even more meaningful. Remember what a broad gesture means? There is a distance between the elbow and the body. The angle at the elbow is more than 90 degrees.

Use of PowerPoint

Slides were used effectively and made the speech more visual. Each slide had either one photo or video, and no text. Slides added value to the speech because they included pictures of art pieces that are difficult to imagine.

Remember that slides should be used only if they improve the audience's experience and include photos, diagrams, or videos of objects or events that are difficult to imagine. An audience can easily imagine a generic house, generic hare, or generic pencil. However, they may not be able to imagine your piece of art or the house where you live.

Add more dialogue

Phil said the words of his neurologist in the form of dialogue:

"The neurologist said, 'Why don't you just embrace the shake?'" It made the speech "Embrace the shake" more lively and engaging.

Phil's speech will become even more alive and engaging if he increases the concentration of dialogue by delivering his thoughts and character's lines in a form of dialogue.

For example:

Instead of "I came home and decided to create something completely out of the box," say "I came home and decided, 'I will create something completely out of the box!'"

Instead of "I decided to ask for 50 cups," say "I decided, 'I will ask for 50 cups'" or "I ordered coffee at Starbucks and asked, 'Could you give me an extra 50 cups?'"

Adding a couple more dialogue lines can increase dialogue concentration and have a significant positive impact on the speech.

Contrast

Phil excellently varied the pace of the speech, gestures, supporting materials, and emotions. Phil can break additional patterns in delivery by varying the volume of his voice more.

Eye contact

Phil maintained eye contact with the audience during the entire speech, even during the slide demonstration. It allowed him to maintain a connection with the listeners, and to keep them engaged.

Summary phrase

Phil's summary phrase was: "Maybe we can remind ourselves every day to cease the limitation." This sentence is an excellent summary of the entire speech. The speech is very succinct and focused. Phil didn't include in his speech any fact or a story irrelevant to the summary phase.

Remember that what is said last is remembered best? The summary phrase was also the last phrase that Phil said. Saying a takeaway message at the end increases significantly the chance that it will be remembered by the listeners.

Phil's speech is an excellent example of how effective building a speech around a summary phrase can be to make the audience think and act differently.

Speech 11: Julia Sweeney has "The Talk"

Access this and other videos used in this book here: https://andriisedniev.com/magicofspeechevaluation

3 foundations of public speaking

Julia tells a story about her daughter and it makes the speech interesting and memorable. Julia is genuine and relives the story on stage.

Is Julia passionate about the topic of her speech? Yes, she is. Through Julia's nonverbal signals it is easy to see how excited she is about her story and this excitement is contagious.

Julia excellently used all 3 foundations of public speaking in her speech.

Use of dialogue

What is perhaps the most remarkable in Julia's speech is use of dialogue.

Firstly, the concentration of dialogue in the speech was high. It allowed audience members not only to hear about the story that happened in the past, but to actually see action develop right in front of them. A right mix of dialogue and narration makes a speech captivating for the audience members.

Secondly, Julia very effectively accompanied dialogue lines by emotional reactions of the characters.

For example:

Daughter: "What? Only females have eggs?" *(Emotion of surprise)*

Daughter: "Mom! Like where you go to the bathroom?" *(Emotion of disgust)*

Julia: "I know." *(Compassion and agreement)*

Nonverbal reactions are much more eloquent than words, and if you accompany dialogue lines of characters with emotional reactions it will increase a positive effect from dialogue several times.

In everyday life during a conversation, people emotionally react to each other's words. When acting out a dialogue you should not only convey the words of the characters, but also their emotions.

A speech where a dialogue is without emotion is as unnatural as a Hollywood movie where characters never look happy, angry, sad, disgusted, scared, or surprised.

The emotional reaction of characters is one of the elements that differentiate a world-class speech from a good one. Always show emotional change in the mood of characters in a dialogue.

Acting out a dialogue

If Damon's speech "Philosophy in prison" was an excellent demonstration of the most common mistakes that people make when acting out a dialogue, Julia's speech is an excellent example of how to act out a dialogue effectively.

When Julia spoke in dialogue on behalf of her 8-year-old daughter, she changed her tone of voice, posture, and emotion slightly. The most important thing in dialogue for the audience to understand is who is talking at each particular moment. If you slightly change your gestures, voice, emotions, or posture, it will be enough for the audience to understand who is talking. If you overact, however, or try to parody another person, it may look silly and unnatural.

If you asked me, "Andrii, could you give a great example of how to act out a dialogue properly?" Julia's speech is certainly one of the examples I would give.

Many people avoid acting out dialogues, even knowing that without dialogue their speech will be far less engaging, because they fear looking silly.

If you want to be a world-class speaker, always include dialogue in your speech, always act out the lines of characters in a form of dialogue, and always show their emotions. Remember that all changes in your voice, posture, and emotions should be slight. If you do, your speech will be natural, captivating, and interesting.

Eye contact

Julia maintained eye contact with the audience during the entire speech. Eye contact allowed her to connect with audience members and to keep them engaged.

Movements

Julia didn't walk on stage during the entire speech. It was very effective, because there were no reasons for her to move. Remember that there are 3 major reasons to move on stage?

Some people think, "To be a dynamic and an engaging speaker I should walk on stage from time to time." If a speaker moves on stage without a reason, it can distract the audience and dilute the power of his or her message. Walk on stage only with a reason and if it makes your speech more visual.

Gestures

Julia's resting position for her hands is perfect. After the end of each gesture, her hands hang relaxed along the body. This natural resting position allows gestures to have bigger amplitude and is the only resting position that doesn't distract the audience.

If you want to make your gestures world-class there are few things that you need to remember: gestures should be broad and open, gestures should be different, gestures should be natural and congruent with a message, hands should return to the natural resting position after the end of the gesture.

Julia's gestures excellently adhered to all these rules. They were natural and helped to make the story more visual. The "Julia Sweeney has 'The Talk'" speech is a good example of effective use of gestures.

Conclusion

Julia's speech didn't have any takeaway message and may have no lasting impact on the lives of the audience members. You may ask, "Andrii, won't Julia's speech become more effective if she adds a conclusion and a takeaway message to her story?"

Actually, no. For entertaining speeches the main goal is to have as many funny moments per minute as possible, not to change anybody's life. Julia accomplished this goal excellently and the audience laughed very often. Entertaining speeches are usually made by comedians, showmen, or professional entertainers.

Public speakers usually make speeches that are both informational and inspirational. Your goal as a speaker is to change the lives of the audience members and to make them think differently. To achieve this goal a speech should have a conclusion and a takeaway message.

Speech 12: Mark Bezos: A life lesson from a volunteer firefighter

Access this and other videos used in this book here: https://andriisedniev.com/magicofspeechevaluation

A perfect story structure

One of the reasons why Mark's story is interesting and engaging is that its structure is very close to the perfect story structure. The speech would become even more effective if Mark introduces a conflict in the beginning clearly and describes what happened in a climax scene in more detail.

Premise

Place: Near a house on fire

People: Mark, another volunteer firefighter, captain of the firefighters, and the woman whose house is on fire.

Premise is effectively introduced in the beginning of the story.

Conflict

Mark wanted to save a living creature and be remembered as a hero. The listeners were able to see the conflict in the story only after Mark's reaction to the fact that another firefighter saved a dog.

If Mark clearly states a conflict right after the premise introduction, says what his goal was, and explains why he decided to become a volunteer firefighter, it will make the story clearer and even more captivating.

Conflict Escalation

Another volunteer firefighter gets a task first and saves the dog. Mark misses this opportunity. Mark is excited to receive his task, but instead of saving a human or an animal he gets a task to bring a pair of shoes from the house on fire.

Climax

Mark receives a letter from the woman whose house was on fire and realizes that the pair of shoes he saved was really important for her and that he did a good deed.

Mark briefly mentioned a letter from the woman and moved on. The climax scene is the most important one in the entire story because a conflict gets resolved and the character learns a valuable lesson that may be useful for the audience. If Mark mentions how he felt after saving the shoes and before receiving the letter, how this letter affected his further work as a volunteer firefighter, or reads exactly what the woman wrote, it will make his takeaway message even more memorable and powerful.

Take your own words seriously

Mark overacted and made faces several times in his speech. For example:

"The dog! I was stunned with jealousy." *(Overacted)*

"Past the 'real' firefighters." *(A gesture with fingers)*

"I know what you are thinking, but I am no hero." *(Overacted and made a funny pose)*

Always respect your own words. Otherwise the audience won't take your message seriously. Audience members may think, "Hey, this guy acts like a clown and doesn't take his own words seriously. If even a speaker doesn't think that what he says is important, why should I accept his advice?"

Mark's speech is interesting, Mark's advice is valuable. If he avoids overacting and making faces, his message will become more memorable and effective.

A summary phrase

"Save the shoes": use of the summary phrase in Mark's speech was very effective.

Firstly, the summary phrase is short and easy to remember.

Secondly, the summary phrase is actionable and specific. After hearing the story, audience members understand what to do, "Help others, now. Even if your help seems as insignificant as saving a pair of shoes it may be very important for people in need."

Finally, all facts and stories in the speech do support the summary phrase. The speech is succinct and focused, which allows a summary phrase to be memorable and potentially change lives of the audience members.

"A life lesson from a volunteer firefighter" is an excellent example of effective summary phrase use.

Dialogue

Mark used dialogue only once in his story, however it significantly helped to make the speech alive and engaging.

"The captain said, 'Bezos, I need you to go into the house. I need you to go upstairs, past the fire, and I need you to get this woman a pair of shoes.'"

Mark also acted out a dialogue very well by changing his own words and gestures just slightly.

By putting lines of other characters in a form of dialogue, Mark can increase the concentration of dialogue in his speech.

For example:

Instead of "Another volunteer came to the captain first and was asked to go inside and save the homeowner's dog," say "Another volunteer came to the captain first. The captain said, 'I want you to go into the house and save the homeowner's dog.'"

Or, instead of "The fire department received a letter from the homeowner thanking us for the valiant effort displayed in saving her home," say something like "The fire department received a letter from the homeowner saying, 'Thank you so much for your enormous effort to save my house and my dog. Someone even brought me a pair of shoes. Everything your team did is so valuable to me and I will remember your good deed forever.'"

Even a couple of additional lines said in dialogue can have significant positive impact on the speech and make it more interesting and captivating.

Speech 13: Eric Mead: The magic of the placebo

Access this and other videos used in this book here: https://andriisedniev.com/magicofspeechevaluation

3 foundations of public speaking

Eric was very passionate about the placebo effect and tricks he demonstrated. Eric was sincere on stage and his goal was to give value to the audience. Eric used experience as a visual anchor to make the speech memorable.

All 3 foundations of public speaking are present in "The magic of the placebo" speech, which makes it interesting and effective.

Anchor

People don't remember what you say, they remember only what they see and feel while you speak. For the point to be remembered, it should be tied to one of the visual anchors: a story, an analogy, or an experience.

Eric used experience as an anchor in his speech. The tricks with a knife and a needle were a very impressive experience and if a point was associated with them it would certainly be remembered.

Eric used effective anchors, but he didn't associate any takeaway message with them. If Eric associated a point with his anchors, the speech "The magic of the placebo" would become more valuable and meaningful for the audience.

If I were to make only one recommendation to Eric, that could have the biggest positive impact on his speech, it would be this, "Make a conclusion after each trick, otherwise the audience members will think, 'Yeah, it was a nice show, however what's the point? We came to learn something new, not just to be entertained.'"

Opening

The first 30 seconds serve as an exam for a speaker because during this time the audience members decide if the speech is worth listening to or not.

Eric began his speech with, "For some time I have been interested in the placebo effect which may seem as an odd thing for a magician to be interested in." Such an opening might not be the most effective way to captivate the attention of the audience.

There are 3 most commonly used openings that are proven to captivate the audience from the first sentence: begin with a story, ask the audience a question, or make a startling statement.

Eric's opening will become much stronger if he begins with a story about research made on the placebo effect. For example, "Several years ago clinic X conducted research on how beliefs of the patients affect their treatment. Patients were given pills made from sugar…"

Filler words

Filler words are words that bear no meaning. Speakers use filler words when they don't know what to say and are not comfortable with silence.

For example, Eric used 12 "ah," 3 "eh," 3 "so," and 1 "well" in his speech. Filler words irritate audience members and make a speaker appear not confident. If Eric completely eliminates filler words from the speech, his delivery will become even more effective.

You might think, "What is the most effective way to eliminate filler words from the speech?" Well, it's easy. If you do use a filler word in a prepared speech, it means you don't know what to say next. If you don't know what to say next, it means you didn't rehearse the entire speech enough at home. To eliminate filler words from a prepared speech, simply practice giving the entire speech at home in front of the wall several times. Once you go on stage you will have internalized the flow and right words will come to your mind at the moment you need them.

If, however, you give an impromptu speech and don't know what to say next, simply pause, think for a few moments and once you are ready – continue. The audience will not notice that you were at a loss for words and you will appear as a confident and sincere speaker.

Acknowledge reactions from the audience

Truly remarkable in Eric's delivery is how he acknowledged reactions from the audience:

"Nice one… Someone who didn't have a childhood is out there."

"Yeah, I know."

"I am sorry. If you are getting queasy, look away."

If audience members see that you hear them and notice their reactions, they will think, "Wow! This speaker really listens to me. I will listen to him." Acknowledgement of reactions from the audience builds connection and turns your speech into a conversation.

Dialogue

Eric used a good concentration of dialogue in "The magic of the placebo" speech. Remember what the rule for dialogue in a speech says? Deliver lines of the characters, your thoughts, thoughts of the characters, and thoughts of the audience members in the form of dialogue.

Eric delivered thoughts of the audience in the form of dialogue. For example:

"I know what people think when they see it, 'Well, he is certainly not dumb enough to stab himself through the skin to entertain us for a few minutes.'"

"People in the back will go, 'Well, if it were real he would be bleeding.'"

All types of dialogue make a speech more engaging and interesting; however, when you say the thoughts of the audience members in the form of dialogue, it also deepens the connection. The audience members may think, "Wow! This speaker really knows what I am thinking. We are on the same wavelength."

Gestures

Eric constantly varied his gestures. The gestures didn't have a pattern and visually supported the speech.

Gestures would become even more meaningful if Eric makes them broader. *(There is a distance between elbow and the body. Angle at the elbow is more than 90 degrees)*

At the end of the gesture Eric often returned his hands to the resting position where they were bent at the elbows and palms stayed at the chest level. This resting position is unnatural, distracts the audience, and limits amplitude of the gestures. Eric's gestures will become more effective and meaningful if he returns his hands to the natural resting position where they hang relaxed along the body.

Contrast

Eric's speech didn't have patterns and his delivery was captivating. Eric varied the pace of the speech, varied gestures, interchanged facts with demonstrations, and spoke with different energy levels.

When a speaker changes all elements of his or her delivery, it's difficult to not be attentive. Eric captivated the attention of the audience for the entire duration of his speech.

Do your homework

Imagine that you hear a speaker saying:

"I don't remember the statistics," "The dosage and the form have something to do with it," or "I'll show it to you some other time when we have slides."

You might think, "Hey, this speaker is unprepared," or "This speaker doesn't know what he is talking about. How can I trust him?"

When you prepare a speech and don't know some statistic, either do research to find it or don't share it with the audience. For example:

Instead of saying "I don't remember the statistics," say nothing.

Instead of saying "The dosage and the form have something to do with it," say "The dosage and the form of a placebo impact how patients perceive effectiveness of the pill." Just don't reveal the fact that you don't know exactly what effect dosage and form have.

If Eric eliminates phrases revealing that he is not prepared, it will make the audience trust his message more.

Speech 14: Meg Jay: Why 30 is not the new 20

Access this and other videos used in this book here: https://andriisedniev.com/magicofspeechevaluation

3 foundations of public speaking

Meg used two stories in the speech, which helped to demonstrate her point and to make it memorable.

Meg's delivery will become even more engaging if she raises her energy. If you are highly passionate about your topic, the audience will be too, but if you speak with low energy the audience may become sleepy and indifferent to your speech.

Meg Jay wanted to change the lives of the audience members for the better. Her speech will become even more sincere if she replaces written language with spoken language. What does that mean? More about it in the next section

Written language vs. spoken language

Imagine that you meet your friend for a cup of coffee and say: "We know that the first 10 years of a career have an exponential impact on how much money you're going to earn."

Your friend may say, "What's wrong with you? Who are 'we'? Exponential impact? Can you talk to me in human language?"

Talk to the audience using the same language you would use in a conversation with a friend while having a cup of coffee. Otherwise, the audience will quickly spot that you don't care about them, you are trying to appear clever, and you are just reading aloud the written script. Once the audience realizes that you are insincere, they will stop being attentive and taking your words seriously.

Meg's speech will become more sincere and alive if she replaces the written language with a spoken one. For example:

Don't say, "When a lot has been pushed to your 30s, there is enormous thirty-something pressure to jump-start a career, pick a city, partner up, and have two or three kids in a much shorter period of time."

Instead say, "Imagine that you have postponed most of your important life decisions to your 30s. Once you really hit 30 you might think, 'Oh, I need to find the love of my life, have kids, and begin a career within only 2 or 3 years.'"

In spoken language tone is more personal than in written language, sentences are shorter, and vocabulary less advanced.

When you create a first draft of your speech, never sit in front of the computer and write. It's a process that writers use and if you follow it your speech will certainly sound like a written article, an abstract from a novel, but not a speech.

If you want your speech to sound conversational, follow a process that speakers use. Create a first draft of the speech by speaking in front of the wall, mirror, or family members. Present the speech in front of the live audience at least once and only then write it down and polish.

Perhaps the biggest mistake you can make on stage is to speak insincerely. To make your speech sincere and conversational, craft a first draft by following a process that speakers use.

Dialogue

Meg used dialogue in the speech, which helped to make her stories engaging and dynamic.

For example:

"And then my supervisor said, 'Not yet, but she might marry the next one…'"

"So what do you think happens when you pat a twenty-something on the head and say, 'You have 10 extra years to start your life?'"

If Meg increases the concentration of dialogue, it will make her speech even more dynamic and engaging. How to increase it? By delivering lines of characters in the form of dialogue.

For example:

Instead of "Alex told me she was there to talk about guy problems," say "Alex said, 'I am here to talk about guy problems.'"

Instead of "Emma came to my office because she was, in her words, having an identity crisis," say "Emma said, 'Meg, I came to you because I have an identity crisis.'"

Dialogue is what makes your speech alive. Dialogue is what allows audience members to see a story unfold in front of their eyes. It's your responsibility as a speaker to reach a healthy balance between dialogue and narration by delivering lines of characters, your thoughts, thoughts of the characters, and thoughts of the audience members in the form of dialogue.

Gestures

Meg used different gestures in her speech and it helped to avoid patterns. Gestures looked natural and supported the speech visually.

Meg will appear even more confident on stage if she uses broader gestures. *(There is a distance between the elbow and the body, the angle at the elbow is more than 90 degrees)*

Broad gestures also convey more meaning than gestures with little amplitude.

In the majority of cases, after finishing a gesture Meg returned her hand to the natural resting position. It allowed her to give gestures bigger amplitude and to avoid distracting the audience.

In the second half of the speech, Meg occasionally returned her hands to the resting position, where her palms were hanging in the air crossed at the stomach level. Meg's gestures will become more effective if she returns her hands to the natural resting position in all cases and avoids the unnatural one that can distract the audience.

Movements on stage

A spot on stage at which you tell a story gets associated in minds of the audience members with this particular story. If you walk over this spot later in a speech, the audience may get confused and stop following your train of thought. If, however, you never walk over this spot again, you can refer to it during the conclusion and the audience will remember your point much better.

Meg's speech will become more visual and clear if she walks on stage with a purpose and uses 3 spots: one spot to tell a story about Alex, one spot to tell a story about Emma, and one spot at the center of the stage to talk with the audience. In this case audience members will clearly understand where a story ends and a conversation begins.

Telling a speech from 3 separate spots will make Meg's speech more clear, visual, and effective.

Make a speech succinct and focused

Meg ends the speech with a summary phrase, "You're deciding your life right now." Remember that if a sentence doesn't help to support a summary phrase, it makes a speech less focused and valuable?

If Meg removes sentences that are not critical for supporting a summary phrase, her speech will become more succinct, focused, and valuable. For example, the following sentences can be removed without subtracting any value from the speech:

"Okay, now that sounds a little flip, but make no mistake, the stakes are very high." Or "I want to change what twenty-somethings are doing and thinking."

If you can convey the same speech in 12 minutes instead of 15 minutes by cutting unimportant sentences, your message will become more memorable and will have a bigger impact on the audience.

Speech 15 Michael Pritchard: How to make filthy water drinkable

Access this and other videos used in this book here: https://andriisedniev.com/magicofspeechevaluation

3 foundations of public speaking

Sincerity and energy

Yes, Michael was sincere on stage. Through nonverbal signals it's visible that he cares about the audience members and truly believes that his invention can make their lives better. Michael is on stage not to sell his product, not to be liked by the audience members, but to give value.

Yes, Michael was passionate about Lifesaver bottle and his energy was contagious.

Anchor

People can remember a takeaway message only if it is linked to a visual anchor: a story, an analogy, or an experience. An experience is a story that happens in front of the audience member's eyes. Michael effectively tied his point to a live demonstration of how the Lifesaver bottle purifies filthy water.

People don't remember what you say, they only remember what they see or imagine while you say it. A creative demonstration made Michael's speech captivating and a takeaway message memorable. While talking about a problem of water shortage or preparing for a weekend in a forest, the audience members may say, "Oh, I remember a demonstration Michael made about how the Lifesaver bottle purifies extremely dirty water. It was impressive."

Opening

The first 30 seconds serve as a preview of the entire speech for the audience. During this time people decide if your speech is worth listening to.

Michael began his speech with: "Good morning, everybody. I'd like to talk about a couple of things today. The first thing is water." These 3 sentences aren't critical to convey Michael's message and they also don't highlight his speech in the best possible way.

The audience members may think, "Yeah. All boring speakers begin their speeches with, 'Good morning, everybody. I'd like to talk to you about…'"

If Michael simply removes these 3 sentences and begins right away with "I see you've all been enjoying the water that's been provided for you here at the conference," his speech will be captivating from the first sentence.

This opening gives the audience a hint that the speech will be about water. Secondly, this opening is personal, unusual, and makes the audience curious about what the speaker will say next.

The first 30 seconds serve as an exam for a speaker. Take them seriously because if you fail this exam the audience will decide that your speech isn't worth listening to, and this opinion will be difficult to change later.

Audience engagement

Michael effectively engaged the audience by letting a cameraman smell water from the pond and letting an audience member taste filtered water.

The audience has an amazing quality that if you engage a single person, everybody feels engaged. If you make audience members a part of your speech, they become more attentive and more likely to accept your messages. Why? Because people will feel like coauthors of your speech.

Michael's involvement of 2 people made his speech more interesting and lively for the entire audience. Always make your speech conversational and don't forget to involve people from the audience wherever it is appropriate.

Pause

Michael used a pause effectively. Whenever Michael made an important point or asked a question, he paused and gave the audience members time to think.

For example:

"What if your water was from a source like this?" *(Pause)*

"While I have been speaking, 4 children have just died." *(Pause)*

People don't change when they listen to a speaker, people change when they think about his or her words. If you want your speech to have any impact, pause after important points, pause after asking the audience a question, and pause after you have finished delivering lines at a fast pace.

Interchange a story with a conversation

Michael's speech is conversational, which not only connects him with the audience, but also makes his speech captivating. In the middle of the speech Michael said:

"I'm sure YOU'LL feel that it's from a safe source."

"Do YOU know it took five days to get water to the Superdome?"

"Do YOU want a drink yet?"

If you ask the audience a question or address the audience, it turns a speech into a genuine conversation. Notice that a common element among all examples above is the word "YOU."

If you want the audience members to be attentive and receptive to your messages, talk to them in a conversation. Asking questions and addressing the audience makes your speech conversational and you an engaging speaker.

Use of PowerPoint

Michael used slides effectively to visually support his speech with pictures. Photos allowed audience members to see what is difficult to imagine and made Michael's words more tangible.

Remember that people can't effectively read the text and listen to a speaker simultaneously? The slides didn't include any text and the audience concentrated their attention fully on the speaker.

Gestures

If Michael uses broader gestures and returns his hands to the natural resting position, his gestures will have bigger amplitude and will become more meaningful.

Remember what it means to make broad gestures? Gestures are broad when at the end of the gesture there is a distance between the elbow and the body, and the angle at the elbow is more than 90 degrees.

To make your speech more visual and body language more effective, use broad gestures and return hands to the natural resting position.

Use of statistics

Michael interpreted statistics, which made it tangible for the audience members. For example:

"This will process 25,000 liters of water; that's enough for a family of four, for three years." People don't know if 25,000 liters is much, but they can clearly imagine a family of 4 and 3 years of a water supply.

Whenever you use statistics in a speech, interpret it for the audience. Make statistics tangible and it will have a much bigger impact.

Promote results

When you pitch a product to potential customers or investors, they don't care about its features, they care about problems it helps to solve.

Michael excellently pitched the Lifesaver bottle. He didn't concentrate on the design of the bottle or the materials it is made from. Michael's message was, "The Lifesaver bottle can save millions of lives by filtering filthy water," and everyone in the audience understood that "saving lives" is a very valuable result.

When you describe a product, concentrate on problems it helps to solve and results it helps to achieve. Audience members will think, "Hey, this product seems valuable because it helps to solve my problem."

How to give high-quality feedback

Several years ago Peter worked as a manager in a major corporation. Peter was very ambitions and dreamed of getting promoted to a director position. To prove that he deserved a promotion, Peter decided to make his team the most effective one in the entire company.

Every week Peter met with each of his 5 employees and gave him or her feedback, "You are not very attentive to details. You don't take enough initiative. I'd like you to set more competitive deadlines for yourself. You don't interact enough with your peers."

After several months, one of the team members, Jack, asked, "Peter, why do you always point out what I did wrong? Why don't you ever express appreciation if I do something right?"

"Jack, you are expected to do your work well and I don't think I should express appreciation when you do what is expected. If you exceed all the expectations, I will certainly acknowledge it."

By the end of the year, all 5 team members decided to not continue to work for Peter. Two of them left the company and 3 moved to other departments. Peter wasn't promoted and within the year his team became less and less motivated and productive.

When you give feedback to another person, it's intuitive to just point at his or her mistakes. Very often the only goal this approach helps to achieve is to make a person you evaluate defensive, unmotivated, and angry at you. You might think,

"Andrii, how should I give feedback to my friends, colleagues, or employees then?"

Scientists who researched successful evaluators figured out that all of them use the same process for giving high-quality feedback. People who use this process manage to change the behavior of individuals who they evaluate much more effectively than those who don't. This process was tested on thousands of people worldwide and gives excellent results 100% of the time. Although high-quality feedback can be applied to any area of improvement, we will review it based on giving feedback to public speakers.

Connect first

For feedback to have any impact you first need to gain trust from the person you evaluate. People accept recommendations only from people who genuinely wish them success and who they feel connected with.

Imagine that you give feedback to Jack. Even before you say the first word, Jack may feel nervous and prepare to defend himself because of the context. Repeat silently, "Jack is the most important person in the world to me. I genuinely wish him success and my only goal is to help Jack to become an even more effective speaker." If you believe this mantra, Jack will certainly sense it and become receptive to your advice.

When you speak, people can easily identify your true intention from the nonverbal signals. Once Jack realizes that you want him to succeed, rather than highlight his imperfections, he will trust you and will listen attentively. The first step in effective feedback is gaining trust from the person you evaluate.

Criticize actions, not a person

Imagine that you get evaluated by someone, "You are stupid. You are impolite. You have poor gestures." Chances are that such feedback won't help you to become more clever, polite, or eloquent but will make you angry at the person who gave it.

Never criticize a person, to avoid engaging his or her emotions, and make your feedback constructive. Evaluate only the actions of the speaker from the observer's point of view.

For example, if you say "I think you speak rather monotonously," Jack will feel that you critique not just his actions but also him as a person. Instead of accepting your suggestion, Jack may become defensive and try to prove that you are wrong.

However if you say "If you change the volume and pace of the speech from time to time, it will add contrast and make the audience even more engaged," Jack will accept your suggestion about how to become more effective on stage.

You can't change a person. You can only help a person change his or her behavior in the future. Never criticize Jack personally. Suggest how changing actions in the future can make him even more successful. If you discuss only Jack's actions, it implies that he can change them in the future, you respect him as a person, and you believe in his ability.

Speak in the past tense

Speaking in the past tense allows Jack to look at his actions from the side, analyze them, and become excited about what he can do even better in the future.

Instead of "You speak quickly and the audience can't really understand you," say "The pace of the speech was too quick and it was difficult to follow the story. If next time you speak a little slower and make more pauses, the speech will be more understandable and memorable."

Consider actions made by a speaker as something already done in the past. Believe in the great future of the person you evaluate and assume that next time he or she will definitely achieve even better results.

Positive first

Tell what Jack did well at the beginning of the evaluation. I know that it's much easier to see mistakes in others but your goal as evaluator is to notice also what a person did well.

Firstly, the positive feedback lets Jack know what he already did well and should keep doing in future. Secondly, positive feedback lets Jack see the results of his efforts and encourages him to work on becoming an even more effective speaker in the future.

The research showed that giving solely negative feedback is a very ineffective way to change behavior. If you give only negative feedback, it can discourage Jack from developing his skills in the future and hit his self-esteem.

If your evaluation begins with things that Jack did well, he will more likely accept and implement your suggestions for improvement.

Make your feedback tangible

Others don't know what you know. Others don't understand what you understand. Instead of just saying "Make broader gestures," show what you mean under "broad gestures." To make each of your recommendations clear and visual, accompany it with an example or a demonstration.

Jack will clearly see what you mean. Jack will realize that implementing a recommendation is possible and will be able to copy your behavior during preparation for his next speech. The more visual and specific your evaluation is, the more impact it will have.

Don't overwhelm

If you give Jack 10 recommendations for improvement, he will not implement any of them. Why? Jack will simply get confused because it's not manageable to improve so many things at a time. He may think, "Why should I even bother to try implementing 10 recommendations? It's simply not feasible."

No matter how many suggestions you have, choose one or two that you will give to Jack. Jack can and will implement one or two recommendations; however, if you give too many, chances are he will get confused and won't work on any of them.

Give Jack one or two recommendations today, one or two during the next evaluation session, and the rest during subsequent evaluation sessions.

Summarize recommendations in the end

People remember best what they hear last. Finish your feedback by summarizing what Jack did excellently and what you recommend to improve during his next speech.

Imagine that you are Jack and hear the following feedback: "Jack, I see that you speak rather monotonously and it makes your speech boring. You need to improve your vocal variety."

If your evaluator used a high-quality feedback process, the same recommendation would sound like this: "Jack, you excellently varied gestures in the speech. You gestured with one hand, with two hands, and sometimes didn't gesture at all. I also noticed that you used both symmetric and asymmetric gestures in your speech. When gestures are varied the audience doesn't see any patterns in them and remains attentive during the entire speech.

"The pace and volume of the speech remained almost the same the entire time. People become less attentive if they notice sameness in delivery. If you vary the pace and volume of the speech occasionally, it will allow you to keep the audience even more engaged. For example… *(Make a demonstration about how to vary volume and pace)*

"Jack, your gestures are strong and make your speech very visual. Try to speak at a different pace and volume next time and your speech will become even more captivating. I am looking forward to hearing your next speech."

Doesn't the second version motivate you more to implement the recommendation? If you truly want your feedback to have a positive impact and make a person you evaluate more successful, remember the following: Feedback should be visual and tangible. Feedback should have more positive points than negative. Don't give more than 2 recommendations at a time. Have genuine intention to help a person you evaluate to become a more successful speaker. Only evaluate actions made by a speaker in the past.

Summarize your recommendations and observations in the end.

How to practice evaluation skills?

I am often asked, "Andrii, where can I find interesting speeches to watch for evaluation purposes?" Actually there are many different sources, but below are 4 of my favorite ones.

TED.com

TED is an organization that hosts conferences all over the world where speakers present ideas from their personal or professional life worth sharing with the world.

TED.com is not only a great source of speeches for evaluation, but also a great place to learn fascinating ideas from different areas of life and get motivated for new endeavors. Among speakers you can find people who have crossed the North Pole, constructed an incredible robot, or even directed world-famous movies.

Igniteshow.com

Ignite show is a geek event held all over the world where people share things that they are passionate about. Each speaker has 5 minutes for a presentation and 20 slides that are automatically switched every 15 seconds. I have been present in person at a couple of such events and also have watched many videos and highly recommend this website.

Commencement speeches

One of the great sources of interesting speeches is commencement ceremonies at major universities. At these ceremonies you can hear commencement speeches from people who have achieved something significant in their lives and give advice to graduating students. Among invited speakers you can find Steve Jobs, Oprah Winfrey, Joanne Rowling, and many others.

On Youtube.com enter "commencement speech + [name of the major university]" and choose a speech you want to watch. For example, "Commencement speech Harvard" or "Commencement speech Yale."

Toastmasters

Toastmasters is an organization with over 200,000 members worldwide that allows speakers to practice 7-minute-long speeches in a safe and friendly atmosphere.

A typical Toastmasters club meeting includes 3 prepared speeches, evaluation, and impromptu speaking sessions. In Toastmasters you can give a 3-minute-long evaluation to one of the speakers in front of the audience and practice not only giving evaluations, but also public speaking skills.

I highly recommend you visit www.toastmasters.org, find a club that is closest to you, attend one of the meetings as a guest, and decide if you want to become a member.

After you watch speeches as an evaluator, successes and failures of other speakers become part of your experience. When preparing a speech you will know exactly what to avoid and how to apply public speaking techniques in different situations.

By evaluating the speeches of others you can make your way to becoming a world-class speaker significantly shorter. Occasionally watch TED.com, Igniteshow.com, or commencement speeches, or visit a Toastmasters club. These resources are excellent for polishing evaluation skills and finding ideas for your future speeches.

Next steps

If you liked this book you will also like *Magic of Public Speaking: A Complete System to Become a World Class Speaker*. *Magic of Public Speaking* system is based on techniques used by the top 1,000 speakers in the world. By using this system, you can unleash your public speaking potential in a very short period of time. *Magic of Public Speaking* excellently complements *Magic of Speech Evaluation*.

I also highly recommend you read *Magic of Impromptu Speaking: Create a Speech That Will Be Remembered for Years in Under 30 Seconds*. In this book, you will learn how to be in the moment, speak without preparation, and always find the right words when you need them.

To learn more recent tips and techniques I encourage you to visit my website at www.MagicOfPublicSpeaking.com.

Final words

I hope that by now you can look at each speech and see which elements were done well and which could be improved. An ability to split a speech to components and look at each of them separately makes you not only a better evaluator, but also a more experienced speaker.

If you can see what other speakers do well and not so well in their speeches, you can easily see it in your own ones. Each time you prepare a new speech look at it from the evaluator's perspective. What did you do effectively? What could you have done better? Follow your own recommendations and your speech will be world-class even if you are giving it for the first time.

This is a final stop in our short tour through *"Magic of Speech Evaluation."* I wish you a lot of fun and success on the rest of your trip through the magic world of public speaking.

Biography

At the age of 19, Andrii obtained his CCIE (Certified Cisco Internetwork Expert) certification, the most respected certification in the IT world, and became the youngest person in Europe to hold it.

At the age of 23, he joined an MBA program at one of the top 10 MBA schools in the USA as the youngest student in the program, and at the age of 25 he joined Cisco Systems' Head Office as a Product Manager responsible for managing a router which brought in $1 billion in revenue every year.

These and other experiences have taught Andrii that success in any endeavor doesn't as much depend on the amount of experience you have but rather on the processes that you are using. Having dedicated over 10 years to researching behavior of world's most successful people and testing a variety of different techniques, Andrii has uncovered principles that will help you to unleash your potential and fulfill your dreams in a very short period of time.

Magic of Public Speaking
A Complete System to Become a World Class Speaker

The Magic of Public Speaking is a comprehensive step-by-step system for creating highly effective speeches. It is based on research from the top 1000 speakers in the modern world. The techniques you will learn have been tested on hundreds of professional speakers and work! You will receive the exact steps needed to create a speech that will keep your audience on the edge of their seats. The book is easy to follow, entertaining to read and uses many examples from real speeches. This system will make sure that every time you go on stage your speech is an outstanding one.

Magic of Impromptu Speaking

Create a Speech That Will Be Remembered for Years in Under 30 Seconds

Magic of Impromptu Speaking is a comprehensive, step-by-step system for creating highly effective speeches in under 30 seconds. It is based on research of the most powerful techniques used by winners of impromptu speaking contests, politicians, actors and successful presenters. The book is entertaining to read, has plenty of examples and covers the most effective tools not only from the world of impromptu speaking but also from acting, stand-up comedy, applied psychology and creative thinking.

Once you master the system, you will grow immensely as an impromptu public speaker, become a better storyteller in a circle of friends and be more creative in everyday life. Your audience members will think that what you do on stage after such short preparation is pure magic and will recall some of your speeches many years later.

The Business Idea Factory

A World-Class System for Creating Successful Business Ideas

The Business Idea Factory is an effective and easy-to-use system for creating successful business ideas. It is based on 10 years of research into idea-generation techniques used by the world's best scientists, artists, CEOs, entrepreneurs and innovators. The book is entertaining to read, has plenty of stories and offers bits of wisdom necessary to increase the quantity and quality of ideas that you create multiple times. Once you begin applying strategies described in this book, you will create successful business ideas regularly and make your life more adventurous. You will realize that there are few things that can bring as much joy and success in business as the moment when an excellent idea comes to your head.

Printed in Great Britain
by Amazon

48043965R00077